You Are Made for More!

LARGE PRINT EDITION

God Made Me More

Promises That Are True

*I am God's masterpiece, created for a purpose and destiny.
I am made for more than surviving life. I will thrive in life.
God is at work in my life and he will perfect
everything that concerns me.
I have a good and bright future.
God is turning my scars into stars.
I am strong, overcoming, and soaring over every obstacle.
God can and will bring me to a flourishing finish.
God is bringing my dreams to pass in his perfect timing.
I am bold and courageous to act against fear.
I am safe in my Father's hands.
I am letting go of the past and moving forward with God.
I choose to wear God's labels: CHOSEN, ONE OF A KIND,
BLESSED, HIGHLY FAVORED, and SUCCESSFUL.
I am a Triple A person: appointed, anointed, and
approved by God.
I will never give up because God has victory
in store for me.*

You Are Made for More!

How to Become All You Were Created to Be

LISA OSTEEN COMES

with a Foreword by Joel Osteen

Faith Words®

New York Boston Nashville

LARGE PRINT EDITION

Faithwords
Hachette Book Group
237 Park Avenue
New York, NY 10017

www.faithwords.com

Faithwords is a division of Hachette Book Group, Inc.
The Faithwords name and logo are trademarks of Hachette Book Group, Inc.

The Hachette Speakers Bureau provides a wide range of authors for speaking events. To find out more, go to www.hachettespeakersbureau.com or call (866) 376-6591.

The publisher is not responsible for websites (or their content) that are not owned by the publisher.

Printed in the United States of America

First Edition: January 2012

Hard Cover ISBN: 978-0-446-58420-3
Trade Paperback ISBN: 978-0-446-58419-7
Large Print ISBN: 978-1-455-52890-5

To the love of my life, Kevin,
and our beautiful children: Catherine,
Caroline, and Christopher

Contents

Foreword
She's More than My Sister

Lisa Osteen Comes is an amazing woman full of faith, joy, and integrity. She is not only my sister, but in many ways she is a hero to me as well. While, like me, she was born into a wonderful faith-filled family, she is no stranger to the curveballs that life can throw our way. Throughout her life she has faced many trials that have tested her faith and her joy. From life-threatening illness to the loss of people she loved, her story is the story so many of us share.

In this book Lisa will take you through her many life experiences in such a way as to intrigue you, entertain you, and inspire you. Her writing style is beautiful and descriptive and once you begin reading you will find it difficult to put down. As you turn these pages you will discover that it doesn't matter how strong your faith is or how much you may desire to do the right thing, you will still be tested. You will see that this is not a sign of weakness, but a sign that

you are human. Above all, however, you will discover
what it means to overcome and to emerge stronger
than you were before.

Lisa inspires me, and she will inspire you too. You
can take to heart every lesson she has learned and
through them you will discover how to recapture
your joy, renew your faith, and respond to every test
with integrity.

Having her in my life has made me a better person,
and I promise, if you take her lessons to heart, you too
will achieve things that you never thought possible. I
urge you to open your heart and your mind and allow
her to share with you the wisdom and advice that she
has always shared with me.

—*Joel Osteen*

Introduction
Made for More

"You've encountered many struggles in life, so I can only think that God must have big plans for you."

My father said this to me after I suffered the initial shock of receiving unexpected divorce papers in the mail. My first challenge in life was surviving a birth defect similar to cerebral palsy. My dad believed, despite all my many trials and disappointments, discouragements and traumas, that I was made for more—more good, more fulfillment, more meaning and purpose. So much more.

He knew that just because I'd known tragedy I wasn't a tragic figure, that just because I had a marriage that failed I wasn't a failure, that even though I'd suffered loss I wasn't a loser. He knew the things that happened to me didn't define me by their harshness or ugliness, their disappointment and despair. No, he knew I was more than all that and, if anything, my circumstances made more clear my resilience and tenacity, my promise and hope—all I was made for and all I am becoming.

My Heavenly Father knows that about you, too.

No matter what you are going through, he sees so much more than the circumstances. He sees that you are made for more goodness and hope, a promise of more than what you are now or how others would limit you to be, because he made you for more, for his pleasure and his good. He made you not only to be more, but to find more: more security beyond the mounting bills and empty bank accounts, more purpose and meaning beyond jobs lost or work that seems unappreciated and pure drudgery, more friendship than what you experience when someone you love isn't there when you need them most, more love than the betrayal or unrequited affection or hurt and disappointment you have now. God waits to love you like no other and give you love that is sure and everlasting, stronger than even death,[1] because he is all about more and designed you to be more, too.

Of course, if you're like me, you may not see that right now. You may need some sign, some big flash of lightning or writing in the sky to show you what more there is, why it's not only okay but good to not be satisfied with enough. You may be waiting for some hidden message that reassures.

I've been there. I've been weighed down till I've had

enough of discouragement and despair, but I realized that God didn't expect me to stay in despair because I was made for more than that.

I was made for victory.

And so are you.

1
Finding More When Things Explode

Because You're Made to Hope

∽

Some days you never forget, though they just might begin typically enough. January 30, 1990, was one of those days for me. Getting ready for work, I had second thoughts about the cotton skirt and blouse I'd chosen to wear. That was strange enough. I'm one of those people who likes to pick out their outfit the night before. I like to be prepared. So why I changed my mind, I still don't know. But that impulse to go back to the closet and change into my black leather skirt and jacket would make a difference for the rest of my life.

At the office, I began to sort through what seemed the usual stack of mail. This was one of my responsibilities in 1990 as director of ministries at my parents' church, Lakewood. I'd been working for my parents since 1983 and always opened their personal mail. Sometimes people poured out their hearts in letters to my parents, requesting prayer. Many people sent encouraging letters, thanking my parents for their ministry. Inmates often wrote, requesting Bibles and other helps. It was not out of the ordinary for my parents to receive speaking invitations and gifts: sermon tapes, books.

That morning, one small package, smaller than a shoe box, caught my eye. A package itself wasn't unusual. I was used to opening packages. But the address stood out a little, typed as if on an old-fashioned typewriter. To "J.O.", it said.

Oh, I thought. *A gift for my dad.* My father, Pastor John Osteen, often received gifts. He was beloved. So I couldn't resist, because boxes are more fun to open than a letter. I lifted the box, which was heavy, as if full of rocks, and shook it like a kid trying to guess what was inside.

Rattle. Rattle, rattle.

"Hmm," I said to myself. "Maybe some cassette tapes from a preacher or singer wanting Daddy to give a listen and his approval."

Then I hesitated. I put down the little box. I didn't have much time because I was getting ready to meet with one of our volunteer leaders.

A few moments later, however, I picked up the package again.

Then put it down.

Then picked it up again.

Three times that morning the package was in and

out of my hands. The box seemed interesting to me because of its heaviness. But there were people I needed to meet with, to-dos to get done, business to tend and finish. The clock kept ticking.

Still, I was like that proverbial cat, curious, and I kept circling the desk, coming back to the package one more time. Finally I gave the box a good shake, and irresistibly tore at the brown wrapping paper.

The last thing I remember was tugging on one little piece of tape that held down the flap of the lid…

No Ordinary Day

As I tore off that last piece of tape, all the lights went out, at least mine. What seemed the beginning of an ordinary day at work suddenly went dramatically awry.

One minute I was sitting at my desk, opening on my lap what I thought was a gift. The next, I was waking from a numbing, then searing, blackness, standing across the room, about six feet from my desk. I have no recollection of leaving my chair, but I was sprawled against the wall.

From head to toe, my body shook violently. I thought: *Have I been electrocuted? God, am I dying?* I suddenly came to my senses and realized I was very much alive. Black smoke smoldered from my clothes, as if I'd been lit on fire. A chemical smell filled my nostrils, and the metallic taste of blood coated the inside of my mouth.

Tucked back in an office off the hallway, with the door still closed, I felt far from everyone at the church that day.

In fact, I was. My fellow coworkers heard a boom, but couldn't pinpoint the source of the noise. No wonder. Our building was large, with offices around the perimeter. In the foyer, some thirty feet from my office, our receptionist Lois was answering phones and helping a half dozen people waiting to chat with different staff members. She heard the blast and thought, *How did someone get a gun in here?* And yet, she would tell investigators later, she somehow knew the loud bang wasn't a firearm.

Other staff members felt the same confusion. They, too, heard a blast but couldn't figure out what might have caused it, or even where it came from within the building. Renee, my father's executive assistant, remembers hearing what sounded like an eighteen-wheel truck, going seventy miles per hour, slamming into the side of our office building. But there was no truck, no scene of a vehicle crash. As staff members sensed something wasn't right, but didn't know what, they began to comb the offices and sanctuary.

Lois ran down a long hallway from the reception

desk toward the noise she'd heard. By the time she made it to my office, I was already across the hall, about fifteen feet away in the office of our accountant, Phyllis.

I had first stumbled to the office next to mine, screaming, "A bomb! It's a bomb!"

My office neighbor stared at me. I'll never forget the look on her face. She sat motionless with her mouth agape, almost catatonic.

I remember thinking, *Okay, I'll try someone else*—something we've joked about since, that she never said a word nor lifted a finger to help me and I was quite a sight to see. (Later, we both realized she was in complete shock.)

At the time, no one thought the noise they heard was a joke. Lois frantically tried to focus through the smoke that was billowing into the hallway. She found me standing with smoldering pieces of paper in my hair, and Phyllis pulling off my jacket and leather skirt, the ones I'd changed into as a second choice that morning. Tiny embers covered the skirt, threatening to ignite into flames. If I'd been wearing the cotton outfit I first had on that morning, I'd surely have been on fire already.

I remember screaming, "It's a bomb! A bomb exploded in my lap!" And then, "Did anything get on my face?"

It's a question any woman would ask. I laugh, thinking, *Yes, things can be going up in smoke and we still want to make sure we look good.*

TO HELP YOU MORE

Develop a Strong Spirit

I'm so grateful that I didn't panic when that mail bomb exploded in my lap. I remained calm during and after the explosion. How did that happen?

I believe over the years, from work on my spirit, God poured his strength into me for my time of need. The Bible tells us that a healthy spirit conquers adversity (Proverbs 18:14), and helps us build our spirits so we can be strong in trials. Proverbs 4:20–23 guides us these three ways:

- **Guard your ears.** Drown out the negative voices in your life. Listen to the teaching of the Word of God; meditate upon God's thoughts about you, think what they mean in your life. Fill your atmosphere with uplifting music.
- **Guard your eyes.** Take time every day to read a portion of the Bible, which will set the pace

for your day. As you read, you will receive en-couragement, strength, and wisdom—and it is always there for you.

- **Guard your heart.** As the proverb says, "Everything you do flows from your spirit." What you put into your spirit, mind, and life is what will come out in the time of trouble. Ask yourself, "Am I allowing negative input into my life?" Replace anything negative with something positive. Be sure to spend time with people pursuing goodness. Find a good local church where you can grow spiritually. If you can walk, do so, even around the block or down the hall; you'll reap the energizing benefits of endorphins. Get into nature and witness God's handiwork—see what fresh air and the beauty of creation will do for your ideas and sense of gratitude.

The health of your spirit directly affects your mind, emotions, and physical body. Taking these practical steps daily will strengthen every area of your life and help you through times of trouble.

Phyllis helped me stretch out on the floor, then

tried calming me and maybe herself, too. "You're going to be all right," she said. "We are going to take care of you." Between reassurances, she told a staff member to call 911 and my parents. Everything seemed like a dream, a nightmare, as faces appeared and receded from the smoke still wafting through the offices.

Though my ears were ringing from that deafening sound Renee described, I heard Lois telling my parents, "Lisa is all right, but she's been in an explosion. She does have some injuries on her leg and abdomen."

Miraculously, in all the chaos, the only pain I remember was my left thumb, burned, bloodied from a one-inch-long split, and throbbing. With all the other injuries, the only one I really felt was my thumb.

No Ordinary Events

Meanwhile, the commotion continued. The building was being evacuated. People were rushing, running out of the building. About sixty staff members and visitors poured from Lakewood Church as groups of others swarmed in: Houston police and firefighters, emergency medical teams, even postal inspectors. An ambulance arrived within ten minutes, yet the chaos played out as if in slow motion. The minutes seemed almost hours.

Paramedics lifted me onto a gurney, then into the

ambulance, and one leaned close.

"Lisa," he said, "as soon as we close the door, I am going to pray for you."

God knew exactly who and what I needed. This man and his prayers brought such peace and calmness to me. I believe in divine appointments and this surely was one.

The paramedic and I prayed together—and I continued to pray the rest of the way to Memorial Hermann Hospital. Even though I was in shock, and the ambulance was racing, bumping along, I prayed quietly the entire ride.

At the hospital, I was lifted out of the ambulance and wheeled on a gurney into Emergency. Within seconds, nurses and doctors clustered round me, cutting off my remaining clothes, asking all sorts of questions, pouring cold fluids over my wounds. I was being pricked and prodded all over.

"Her injuries are not nearly as bad as the paramedics described," I heard one man say. I was covered with a blanket as he added, "She may be out of here today."

The paramedic who had prayed for me in the ambulance was nearby when a nurse momentarily removed the blanket. He gasped and looked at his fellow medic, both of whom were the first to tend to my wounds in Phyllis's office and then call in the list of my injuries.

A change had occurred as we prayed together during that twenty-minute ride to the hospital. My wounds—terrible, serious tears and burns on my abdomen and legs—had already begun to heal.

Still the physicians were taking no chances. They prepared to have me transported with a team to Methodist Hospital for treatment. By this time, only my family was allowed to see me, and Kevin, now my husband, whom I was seriously dating at the time. I didn't know it, but media had begun to descend upon and swirl round the hospital, which quickly became tightly guarded.

My close friend Debra barely got in by sheer determination. The security guard had stopped her but she insisted until one of the nurses said, "She looks like the Osteens. Let her in!"

Kevin, who had listened to radio reports already being broadcast as I was on my way to the hospital, was shaken upon seeing me in Emergency. I'll never forget how he turned away and wept.

Back on a gurney and on my way into another ambulance, I could see clusters of people, journalists and newscasters, gathering to ask me questions as I was wheeled into the second hospital that day. Reporters from the *Houston Chronicle*, and radio, even CNN, were there for what would be their lead story, nationwide and around the world, over the next few days: BOMB HURTS PASTOR'S DAUGHTER. LAKEWOOD

CHURCH TARGET OF EXPLOSIVE.

No Ordinary Calm

Looking back, I'm grateful that I didn't panic but instead remained calm during all the chaos. *How did that happen?* you may wonder. *How can anyone find their wits and remain calm in the midst of trauma?*

The Bible says that it is the spirit of a man that sustains him in trouble.[1] This is one of the promises of God: to strengthen us when we feel weak. You may be in the middle of something that has exploded or imploded in your life. But even now you can remain grounded, calm, and stable in spite of your circumstances.

God will help you through the dark, hard, low places, and one of the most beautiful psalms in the Bible tells us this.

Psalm 23 has always brought me great comfort. Especially during and immediately after the mail bomb exploded in my lap, the words of this psalm helped me. They comforted me in that very real valley of the shadow of death because they acknowledged five promises from God:

1. You don't have to be afraid, because God is with you

It may seem like you are in a valley of death, but that valley is just a shadow. God is walking with you, guiding your steps out of the valley. Keep following him and he will bring you to a mountaintop, where you can see beauty again and breathe freely.

2. God's rod and staff will comfort you

It's not just for pretty imagery that a rod and staff are mentioned in Psalm 23. A rod is a symbol of authority and a staff is an instrument of support. God offers you both. He has authority over you, and that means no one, nor any thing or situation, can snatch you from his hands.[2] He will support you and hold you up in the valley.

3. God causes you to triumph

Did you know that you can have a triumphant attitude in the valley? You can because the valley is temporary and God is working on your behalf, even preparing a table for you in the presence of your enemies. How beautiful is that—to feast your spirit in the places of emotional famine!

4. God strengthens you to make it

He anoints your head with oil. That means God chooses to be with you, in you, filling you with his strength. Oil represents the Holy Spirit—God's presence in you. The Holy Spirit is your helper, who empowers you to go through the valley and get to the mountaintop. You don't have to walk alone, or do everything in your own strength, which is limited anyway. You can rely upon God's limitless power at work in you, for you.

5. Goodness and mercy will follow you

No matter what you face today, you cannot get away from God's great goodness and mercy. You may be in a dark valley, but the blessings of God follow you wherever you go. You may not think so. For example, you may need a new job, and you pray for God's favor when you interview for one, but you don't get the job. God may have spared you from something that was less than what he designed for you. Believe in his goodness, and rely on his grace, for he is always for you. He is the shepherd who cares for and loves his sheep through every valley, and even when things around you go up in smoke.

TO HELP YOU MORE

You're Safe with the Shepherd

When things around me got crazy and I couldn't understand what was happening or why, Jesus, the good shepherd, led me away from the chaos to a place of peace. He is there to help you through whatever falls apart in your life. He will walk with you through every dark valley.

Psalm 23 shows that you can always count on him to...

- **care for you.** He will go in search of the littlest lamb and give total care to the entire flock. I love how the Bible describes that he gathers the lambs and carries them close to his heart (Isaiah 40:11), does not let the flock want, and watches closely over your life.
- **lead you to where you need to be.** He goes ahead of us to find the green pastures. If you are in a place of confusion or chaos, look to the shepherd to guide you to the right place at the right time.
- **give you peace.** The shepherd knows he must find quiet pools of water because sheep will

not drink from a fast-flowing river. They fear water too much. If they fell in, their wool would soak up the water and the river would carry them away like a sponge and cause them to drown. Jesus promises: "Come to me, all you who are weary and burdened, and I will give you rest" (Matthew 11:28). He wants to give you a balanced, peaceful life, not one soaked with hurry, not frantic or freaked out.

- **calm your soul.** The shepherd is always on the lookout for the wolves that prowl, the storms that brew. He promises to stand by you when both creep upon you. He promises to steady you with his strong hand. He will keep your soul.

- **keep you clean and healthy**. Sometimes the shepherd has to apply ointments and other medicines to his sheep to ward off flying pests and parasites. Jesus, our shepherd, anoints our heads with oil—his oil of healing—everywhere it hurts: mind, body, or spirit.

- **never leave you.** Jesus will never forsake us. He promises to dwell with us forever. The shepherd never left his sheep. He will never leave you.

- **call you by name.** You are his sheep and recognize his voice, just as he recognizes yours. He listens for you. He speaks to you (John 10:1–20). He recognizes you. Isn't that powerful? To many people, sheep are sheep. But the good shepherd knows what sets each one apart, makes each one special. He knows every detail of your life, when you rise and when you sleep, what you love and what you loathe. He knows where the black spots are, when an ear is torn, if you're missing any wool. He longs for your company and wants to give you his as he brings you to the place he's prepared for you.

No Ordinary Aftermath

As more and more reporters clamored to report the mail bombing events, I was given a private room on a secure floor in the hospital. Our Lakewood Church security volunteers began to take turns in shifts, guarding my door. They protected me from the media storm and strangers, as did my brother Joel, who stepped in to coordinate all the media questions and interview requests.

They couldn't stop the calls, letters, and flowers that began to flood my room from around the world. The city of Houston and local churches reached out in such a loving way. I will never forget the kind words and prayers from people I'd never even met. Even President George H. W. Bush called. His office made arrangements with Joel to speak to my parents at the hospital. The leader of the free world called to offer his condolences, express concern, and assure us that investigators would do everything possible to find who committed the crime at Lakewood. There was so much excitement over the president's call, and the press was there for the story to make headlines the next day. I always wondered why I didn't get to talk to the president myself, since I was the one injured!

Meanwhile, a series of doctors began to explain the intensity of my wounds. I needed surgery to repair three holes in my abdomen and a larger hole in my right leg that destroyed a portion of muscle tissue. I was expected to be in the hospital for weeks.

Officials from the Alcohol, Tobacco, and Firearms Department and the FBI filed to my bedside as early as the morning after the incident. The seriousness of the crime began to sink in. I was questioned on the explosion itself, the nature of the package, even potential suspects. The clothes I'd worn that day, though burned and torn, were saved by police, and they remain in custody of the FBI today.

Every member of my family was questioned, as were people at our church. Broadcasters and journalists were looking for any new details to report. The attention felt intrusive in all the wrong ways, about my personal health and silly things like office operations.

Over the next thirteen days I underwent surgery and postrecovery. The rapidness of my healing for such serious injuries surprised even the doctors. I will always have reminders: a ten-inch scar, resembling a shepherd's staff, across my stomach, and a five-inch scar and slight indention on my right leg.

Investigators said it was a miracle I survived with just two scars, a miracle that I hadn't been killed. The mail bomb actually malfunctioned. Instead of exploding all over my body as intended, it blew out both ends. That rattle I'd heard when I shook that little brown package at least three times that morning was the rubbing of shrapnel against ten-inch nails— metals that upon explosion drove into my office desk, blasting a significant hole in one drawer, and pocking the walls with gashes, slashes, and holes.

"It was as if someone was standing between Lisa and the bomb," one of the authorities at the scene was quoted as saying.

I knew exactly who that someone was.

No Ordinary God

I got the chance to tell about that someone, beginning with one day in particular. Just after my surgery, Victoria, Joel's wife, showed up to visit me at the hospital. She pulled out some makeup and began to fuss with my hair.

I must have been looking pretty bad, I thought, as she went to work, brushing and styling. After all, my hair hadn't been washed for days. It was long and puffy—big, as we Texas girls like to say—but also full of tiny particles of debris and matter from the explosion. Carefully, patiently, Victoria picked out the pieces of stuff, fixed me up, and made me feel pampered and loved.

Finally she finished. "Ta da," she announced.

I felt better, and it was a good thing, because right then Joel walked in with a video camera.

"Lisa," he said, "the people in the church and city want to know you are all right."

Oh my goodness, I thought. *Sneaky!* But smart, too. Joel knew I wouldn't have agreed to a filmed interview without sending in Victoria first. I was still shaken from everything that happened.

But there was no time for that. Joel and Victoria took me in a wheelchair to a small press conference in the hospital. I wondered what to say. My father was there to help. I felt instant relief when he stepped up to talk, even though it was my picture on the front page of the *Houston Chronicle* the next morning. (Thank goodness for Victoria's skills!)

That press conference was just one of many to come, and a great number of people kept trying to provoke gloom and doom from the bomb explosion. There was all this speculation that I should have been killed by the events that day, that I never should have survived.

"Your daughter is so lucky to be alive," one journalist after another told my father.

"No," he replied. "She is blessed because we serve a good God."

We do.

God has more goodness in mind for us than we can imagine. He designed each of us with a great plan. He made us to do good and to live greatly. He picks up the pieces of our lives. He takes what was shattered and lovingly, patiently, puts things back together. He leads us to the green pastures, beside the quiet waters, because he has great things in mind for us—more than moments of chaos, more than trauma.

I knew this before the explosion. I had read many times God's promise to take even the worst of situations and turn it around for our good and the good of others.[3]

After the explosion, I could count so many ways God did this for me: Was it any coincidence that I felt the impulse to change clothes that fateful morning of the bomb, from a cotton outfit to a leather one? Or that the bomb malfunctioned, causing lesser injuries than might have been possible? Or that the paramedic by my side in the ambulance offered to pray for me? Or that instead of spending weeks in the hospital, my healing was beyond what the doctors expected and I was released in thirteen days?

No.

None of these things were coincidence. These are instances of how God was there when things in my life exploded. They are personal reminders, just like that shepherd's hook-shaped scar that I bear, that for every extraordinary act that man might intend for evil, we have an extraordinary God ready to be right by our side. He's ready to pick up the pieces. He saves what is broken. He makes all things new because he has a plan, a purpose. He is the shepherd with more in mind for his sheep than dark valleys.

God watches over our lives and never slumbers nor sleeps.[4] That means he even works the night shift! No matter what things explode in your life,

God has more goodness in mind for each of us than we can imagine.

God is going to be there. He's going to make a way through the debris for you, just as he did for me. That means he is going to hold you in the dark, even when you don't know that he is there.

Our longtime family friend Gerald Hilley reminds me of this. Many years ago he had heart surgery and during recovery told how he had an unforgettable dream.

In utter despair, he cried out to God in anguish, "God, where are you?"

In answer to his question, a gigantic figure appeared. The figure was holding someone. Gerald moved closer to see who. As he did, he recognized that the tiny figure in the lap of this gigantic figure was himself being held by God. Gerald then heard a voice: *Son, it's not where I am that matters. It's where you are.*

We are in the embrace of God. He always has a hold on us.

I am in the hold of my creator.

So many things in this life will threaten to undo us, but when everything seems to be crashing around you, remember that you, too, are in God's embrace.

That doesn't mean there will never be another struggle or there will never be more strife or that things won't explode or implode in your lap. I struggled after that bomb explosion to go back to a normal schedule and lifestyle. Though my physical recovery amazed even the doctors, it took a little while to feel completely secure again in my own office. For a season I also feared the person who meant my family harm in the first place was still out there, preparing to harm us again.

That was one reason I was delighted when I was contacted by the television show *Unsolved Mysteries*. I was asked to reenact the crime for a mass audience, and I hoped doing so would help investigators with tips to finding the bomber. The program used a documentary-style format to profile real-life mysteries and unsolved crimes, and was hosted by the handsome Robert Stack for fifteen years. Stack's gruff and unmistakable voice became synonymous with the show and made it all the more eerie. Viewers were invited to telephone or e-mail any information that might help solve the crimes.

While 47 percent of the program's cases concerning fugitives led to arrests and mysteries solved, my episode didn't. My short acting debut led to more than five hundred responses with clues and leads, and the episode on the explosion aired numerous times over the next few years, but the crime remains unsolved to this day.

Does that mean God isn't in control?

No. He has opened the door to more for me even through chaos and trauma. He's unfolded a plan for me, just like he will for you, despite awful events and dark valleys. In fact, it is there that he shows up more than ever—and God is always present, always caring.[5]

When that bomb threatened to shatter my faith in the goodness of people, God brought me the well wishes and prayers of those I'd never met. When my hopes of doing good work in ministry threatened to go up in smoke that day, God used the aftermath to give me a larger audience and a taller platform for sharing his love.

Just six weeks after I was released from the hospital, I was speaking at Lakewood. I chose Psalm 23 to focus upon: "Even though I walk through the valley of the shadow of death, I will fear no evil."

I had walked that valley, and God walked with me. Our extraordinary God was there. Wherever we go, he is there.[6] He has his hand upon us, and under us, and out to us. He picks up not just the pieces of our lives when they fall apart around us.

He picks us up, too.

Today, when I say, "The bomb could have destroyed my life, if it were not for the grace of God," I add jokingly, "Instead, I am the bomb."

So are you.

My father was right. We're not lucky to be alive. We're blessed, because we serve a good God.

2
Finding More When You Feel Flawed

Because You're Made a Masterpiece

∽

When I tell you that "you are the bomb"—that is, spectacular—do you believe it? Do you see how special you are, remarkable, meant to be and to do great things, to impact this world in a meaningful way?

So many people don't. They think they are ordinary. They don't see their purpose or have a clear sense that they are made to do something great for God. They resign themselves to less—less fulfillment, less accomplishment, less meaning.

I could have gone through life not seeing how I was made unique and precious to God, made on purpose, for a purpose. After the mail bomb explosion, I could have become stuck by many things. I found myself at a crossroads. Was I going to allow fear to paralyze me, or was I going to believe God had a greater plan for my life? I could actually picture myself spiraling down a deep, dark tunnel of fear. I didn't want that life. That would mean backing away from every great thing God had planned for me.

Have you ever felt stuck? Powerless? Trapped in circumstances, anger, hurt, addictions? Are you backing away from the dreams and desires that are in your heart?

Sometimes others tell us what we aren't, what isn't possible, that we should just accept things the way they are and get on with our lives. More often than not we're that very critic, not allowing ourselves to believe in more. We look at others in a spotlight, or in the chair at the head of a company, or who have worldwide influence and think: *Oh that person has a destiny, but I'm not that important. I'm just a nurse.* Or, *I'm just a salesperson.* Or, *I'm just a waiter. Just a mom. Just a friend.*

The world tried to tell my parents otherwise.

The World Will Always Say You're Less

When my parents took little baby me home from the hospital, they thought everything would be great. That changed within just a few weeks. I couldn't suck or swallow, so I didn't eat well or gain weight. When placed on my tummy, I didn't have the strength to lift my tiny head off the bed. When on my back, I couldn't lift my tiny arms.

Something was wrong. Why weren't my muscles functioning properly?

Concerned, they took me back to the hospital. My brother Paul might have wished this was for an exchange or a return. But, no, my mother and father wanted to get to the bottom of things. Only upon that checkup did doctors realize that the umbilical cord, that lifeline between mother and child, had wrapped around my neck during birth. This restricted the oxygen supply to my brain and caused both brain and body to develop abnormally. The doctors told my parents that my symptoms were similar to a child with cerebral palsy.

"Don't expect Lisa to ever walk or talk normally," one doctor said.

"Prepare," another added, "to take care of her for the rest of your lives."

Any new parent would be devastated by news like that. Some might resign themselves to everything the doctors predicted. Others might determine to turn over every medical rock in a fight for help and answers.

My parents, believing in a destiny given by God and not men, turned to their faith. This was remarkable because my father had been taught that miracles were a thing of the past. But as his faith and relationship with God grew more and more passionate, he began to listen to his heart and to

God, [1] not just to what he had been taught.

His heart told him to pray. So my father and mother prayed for a miracle. They chose to believe that I had a destiny beyond what the doctors expected. Rather than resigning themselves to what everyone around them would have said was reality ("Just accept it." "Just deal with it."), my parents focused on the possibilities. They sought God's divine intervention and prayed for what our maker, not just medicine, could do. They were sure there was more for me than what everyone else was willing to believe.

And nothing happened.

So they prayed more…and, still, there were no flashes of light. No rolls of thunder. No loud voices from Heaven.

Instead there were difficult times. My mother had to force-feed me because I still couldn't swallow well. I had to be held and physically moved by others because I was like dead weight and wasn't moving at all on my own.

Still my parents continued to pray for me, day after force-feeding day. And one morning, I lifted my head from the bed. I'd never done that before. Another day, I began to move my limbs. Again, this was a first. Yet another day, I sat up on my own, as if it was the most natural thing for me to do.

All this happened by my seventh month.

Ecstatic, my parents scheduled another visit with my pediatrician.

Dr. Molly Stevens confirmed my progress, even nicknaming me the Miracle Girl, though she and the other doctors had no explanation for the turnaround. My parents didn't need it. They took my transformation and my normal development growing up as a very direct answer to their prayers. (Of course, my brothers, Joel and Paul, would question whether I was normal or not. Brothers! You've got to love 'em.)

For me, and for my parents, my recovery was a life-changing event. My miraculous turnaround inspired my father to change the course of his ministry and his life. Because of his and my mother's so-

> *God tells us that he made us on purpose, for a purpose, not just to exist but to be his masterpiece.*

lidified belief in the power of miracles, they decided to start Lakewood, a church that believed in miracles.

I like to think, then, that as the Miracle Girl I was Lakewood's founding member! Really, I was just the first of many miracles to come. Today Lakewood is the largest church in America, where I am honored to serve as an associate pastor of a congregation led by my brother Joel and his wife, Victoria.

Oh, and our church family will tell you, when I'm on the stage to speak, I walk and speak just fine.

God Will Always Say You're More

The truth is you don't have to be perfect or remarkable from the moment of your birth. You don't have to be called into a spotlight, a president's chair, or a ministry to be a person of destiny. You can be ordinary or an outsider, flawed and failed, tried or tired. No matter what shape you're in or how you began or where you are now, God will use anyone from any walk of life to fulfill his plans and purposes. He's renowned, in fact, for choosing the ones others would call a mess or miserable, the ne'er-do-well, the nobody.

To God, every person is someone special. Each person is his creation. He tells us that he made us on purpose, for a purpose, and not just to exist but to be his masterpiece. A whole chapter in the Psalms[2] describes how before we were formed in our mother's wombs, all the days of our lives are written in his book.

TO HELP YOU MORE

You Can't Keep Away Your Destiny

As a twenty-year-old, Kevin worked hard week-days and on weekends partied with friends. He believed in goodness and decency. He was living life to the fullest. Or so he thought.

Something was missing, but he wasn't sure what. He just knew he didn't want to remain in the same cycle of work-work-work-and-party-on-weekends. Something inside told him that he was made for more than that.

Kevin hadn't attended church much in his life, but a friend told him about God for the first time, and Kevin wanted to know more. He bought a Bible and began to sleep with it under his pillow. Having the Bible near gave Kevin comfort, though he couldn't explain why. Sometimes he would fall asleep with that Bible held tightly to his chest. During this time, he began to attend the only church familiar to him, but he recognized quickly that he could not relate to anything being said or done there.

Later some friends told Kevin that he could know God like a friend—and God had an amazing plan for every person's life. This was what Kevin was looking for, not ritual or religion but relationship with the one who made him, and made him for a purpose.

If someone had told me that grabbing a Bible and sleeping with it could lead to a passionate relationship with God, I might not have believed it. But God works in amazing ways to get us to our destinies. He can use a Bible under the pillow just like he can use a friend and that ache for more inside each of us.

Today Kevin serves Lakewood Church.

When he tells this story, I still marvel because I see how God prepared my husband for me. Kevin is the husband I prayed for as a young woman, the husband who would not just want to live a life for himself, but be a blessing to others.

Isn't that amazing?

God knew you before you were born.

God knit together your destiny as he knit together your very bones.

Your genetic makeup, personality, talents, and the family you were born into all happened by the hand of God, not by chance. God actually designed you for your destiny. He created you with the exact gifts and callings that you would need and set you in the right family. He determined every detail about your being and all of your days too. He has written them out in his great book.

That's right. God, the best-selling author of all time, the author of the universe, has a story just about you, one just about me. He calls us his workmanship. When he created you, he declared you a work of art, significant to him, important. He put his stamp of approval on you and sent you out into the world to show you off. *See,* he says, *I created this beautiful one. This one is good, for good works I've prepared in advance. My signature is all over this one. This one is made by my hand, sent just for me.*[3] I imagine that he thinks, *Wow! I did a great job! Isn't she wonderful! Isn't he amazing! See my masterpiece!* He is excited for you to do all he made you to do, be all he designed you to be. That means you are important because he has a special assignment just for you, and someone needs what only you have. You are important because your life has an everlasting impact in the world around you.

I think we miss how remarkable that is. *His* masterpiece. God's *masterpiece.*

Why do so many of us have trouble believing that?

Because God Made You Priceless

Too many of us remark at how when God created the heavens and earth, each day he stepped back and marveled at what he made. He said, "It is good."[4] The earth and waters, the fish and fowl, the beasts, the flora and fauna, sun and moon, night and day, the stars—they're all good, as decreed by God.

Why don't we believe in our bones that when he created us, he stepped back and marveled in the same way, "This is good." *He is great. She is incredible.*

If we did believe, wouldn't we wake in the morning with our first thought about our destiny and what we would do for God with the gift of another day? We would think, *God, direct my steps today so that I will fulfill your purpose for my life.*

Instead too many of us dread our days, and we both lie down and rise up with all kinds of anxious or negative thoughts. We don't believe in the remarkableness of our own lives.

But each life—your priceless life—is a masterpiece nonetheless.[5]

Think about masterpieces today. One of the most valuable and famous paintings in the world is the *Mona Lisa* by Leonardo da Vinci. The actual painting, valued at more than $713 million (in 2010), hangs on display in the Louvre Museum in Paris. Though we see copies of it, and sometimes large ones, the original is quite small, just 30 inches by 21 inches in size.

When you look at the *Mona Lisa*, the painting is beautiful, but the woman? Really, she's not all that.

She could use a day in the salon. I mean, honestly, someone needs to get ahold of that hair!

While we can laugh about that, it's no joke that whatever you think of the woman's appearance doesn't affect her value one bit. She is the original painting by the famous artist Leonardo da Vinci.

I think about my longtime friend, Bebe. She is beautiful inside and out. Her hair always looks fabulous and her clothes beautifully put together. But that is not what makes her valuable. What makes her priceless is that she is an original, a masterpiece created by God himself—authentic, one of a kind, impossible to duplicate, created to fulfill her destiny. That is what makes her of great worth on both earth and in Heaven.

But every masterpiece is a work in the making. Even the *Mona Lisa* was made over time and with layers of paint and work, the manipulation of dark and light pigments. You, too, are in the making, and your maker is at work on your destiny right now. Are you opening yourself to the mix that will make your life into more—something priceless and remarkable?

Stir Your Destiny

How do you open yourself to his making? What does stirring up that sense of destiny mean in everyday life?

1. Recognize you are not stuck

You may be in a place where you feel stuck. You find yourself sinking into hopelessness and despair, accepting that things will never change or get better. I can definitely relate. You can't see the way out, nor any light at the end of the tunnel. But I want you to know that just because you can't see the way out, or you can't seem to do anything about your situation, doesn't mean you are stuck.

What you can't do, God can do.

The first step is to recognize this very truth: when your ability ends, God's ability begins. His grace is sufficient to help you get unstuck. Isn't that a relief? You can take a deep breath right now and say, "I am not stuck because God is helping me!"

The Bible says, "No test or temptation that comes your way is beyond the course of what others have had to face. All you need to remember is that God will never let you down; he'll never let you be pushed past your limit; he'll always be there to help you come through it."[6] One version of the Bible puts it this way: God will show you the way of escape.

Don't settle for less. Instead, reach for more from God. Expect him to help you. In Proverbs 2:7, God reminds us that he holds victory in store for us.

God's plan includes success, fulfillment, and purpose. His plan also includes overcoming any obstacle and adversity that you may face in life. Absolutely nothing you have encountered is too difficult for him.

2. Pursue God and his plans for your life

God will not just pick you up one day and put you into your destiny. You have to take steps toward it and know that God will direct those steps.[7] He will teach us to number our days so that we may gain hearts of wisdom.[8] He promises to give us discernment and focus to see exactly what he calls each of us to do.[9] Begin to ask God to help you right now wherever you are. God invites you to come to him: "If any of you lacks wisdom, you should ask God, who gives generously to all without finding fault, and it will be given to you."[10] God so longs to help you.

Doing this can be as simple as saying, "Father, I'm available to you. More than anything else, I want to do your will. I want your wisdom and direction in my life." Prayers like this will keep the sense of destiny in the forefront of your thinking and will keep your heart in the position to receive his very best for you.

TO HELP YOU MORE

Eight Promises about Your Destiny

1. Psalm 16:11: God will make known to you the path of life.
2. Psalm 31:14–15: Your times are in his hands.
3. Psalm 25:12: God will instruct you in the way chosen for you.
4. Psalm 57:2: God will fulfill his purpose for you.
5. Psalm 121:7–8: God watches over your life.
6. Psalm 145:18–19: God will fulfill your desires.
7. Psalm 37:23–24: God will direct your steps.
8. Isaiah 48:17: God will show you what to do and where to go.

3. Know God will prepare you

Moses was designed for his destiny, even though he couldn't see it at first. God called him to go back to Egypt and lead the Israelites out of captivity. But Moses didn't feel ready or able. He said, "God, who am I that I should go to Pharoah and bring them out?"[11] He then gave God every excuse about why he couldn't do it, He had a speech impediment. He wasn't perfect. He had killed a man in an attempt to defend an Israelite slave.

God wasn't concerned about any of Moses's weaknesses. He told Moses, *You just tell them who sent you. It's not about you, Moses. It's about me. What matters is who I am, not who you are.*

God is saying the same thing to us today: *Don't worry about what you don't have. Don't worry about what or who you aren't. I am all you need. I am your strength and protection, your wisdom and provision. I am with you wherever you go.*

God has a track record of calling people to do things beyond what seems their natural ability. Look at David in the Bible, a shepherd boy who defeated a giant, the enemy of his people, and then became king. Look at Peter, a hotheaded, unschooled fisherman, who became a respected apostle in the Church.

It's easy to feel unqualified and overwhelmed, even when you know in your heart what you are called to do. But that feeling of inadequacy is good. That means you know you need God, and you can't fulfill your destiny without him.

God isn't looking at your faults or weaknesses. He looks at his ability to work through you. He invests in you, molds you, and prepares you, using every experience you have and redeeming everything for something good. That means every season in your life has a purpose. It is training ground. Even when you can't see it, God is at work, adding to you, shaping you. You are growing in faith and being prepared for your next step.

David couldn't be king without understanding how sheep needed a shepherd.

Peter couldn't have become a strong leader without being rough, tough, and unmovable—eventually in faith—like a boulder.

Moses couldn't lead the people without witnessing the horrors of slavery, and God redeemed his bad act of killing a guard by letting him lead a multitude to new life.

4. Understand your desires are connected to your destiny

When I look back on my life, I see clearly that God placed desires inside my heart. As a teenager, I desired to study the Bible. As a young adult, I began to think about preaching and wishing I would serve others by sharing the good news of God. These desires were not random wishes. They were from God. The desire to preach certainly had to be from God, because I was once too nervous to speak in front of people!

Yet I didn't always recognize the path of destiny God had prepared before me. Too often, it's easy to think, *I don't know what it is that God wants me to do.* But if you search your heart for what you like to do, you'll see that God has placed desires in you. Do you like to help the needy? Do you enjoy encouraging others? Maybe you like to fix things for people or provide for them and serve them. No matter what your vocation, God wants you to be involved in using your gifts to help others and influence your world. Desires like these are part of the destiny he has for you. The fact is you are his ambassador, his hands and feet, wherever you go. He is calling you to do great things for him.

I encourage you to list on a piece of paper all of your heart's desires. Look at the list. Talk to God about these things. Listen for him. Act upon some of the desires. See what happens!

5. Take confidence in the fact that nothing and no one can keep you from your destiny unless you allow it

How easy it is to become impatient. We tend to want everything right now, but God has a right timing for us, and it may be later. First, there may be obstacles to overcome, or persecution and opposition. But God promises in the Bible, "Many are the plans in a man's heart, but it is the Lord's purpose that prevails."[12]

That means something may go awry in your life. You may fail a board exam the first time. You may lose a fortune and struggle to earn a living. You may have health challenges.

That doesn't mean that you cannot fulfill your destiny.

No one or nothing can stop God from fulfilling your destiny.

You are the only one who has the power to stop and give up.

Isn't that freeing? God is bigger than any mistake, every setback, all opposition.

No matter what has happened in your past, you have not missed your destiny. No person or negative event can stop you from fulfilling your purpose, but it's up to you to keep going.

The Bible encourages: "You were running a good race. Who cut in on you and kept you from obeying the truth?"[13] Don't let anyone or any circumstance cut off your pursuit of your destiny or stop you from running your race. Anytime you feel tempted to give up, remind yourself, "I am not going to let anyone or anything stop me. I have a destiny to fulfill. This set-back is only temporary. I am God's masterpiece and he will get me to that finish line."

That is what God wants us to see, He has a destiny for us, and we only have to reach for it and grab hold of it. Even my young son showed me the truth of that.

Live Expectantly

Not long ago, our young son, Christopher, called me at the church. "Mom, when are you going to be home?" he asked excitedly.

"I'm on my way now," I told him.

"How long?" he pressed.

"Soon," I said.

"No," he persisted. "How many minutes?"

"About two minutes."

"Mom, I'm going to look out the window for you."

"Okay," I said, "Bye—"

"Wait, Mom," he said before I could hang up. "Which side of the house will you be coming from—the left or the right?"

He was serious about this. He wanted to see me driving up the street and turning into the driveway. He wasn't just waiting for me. He was looking for me with expectancy, great expectancy.

There's a difference!

Are you living with that kind of expectancy, the kind that looks out the window to see from which side God's goodness will come to you?

Believing and expecting are keys to fulfilling your destiny, to living it. God's put his word on it, too. He says, *I will instruct you in the way chosen for you.*[14] He says in Jeremiah 29:11–14, one of my favorite passages, "For I know the plans I have for you, plans to prosper you and not to harm you, plans to give you a hope and a future. Then you will call upon me and come and pray to me, and I will listen to you. You will seek me and find me when you seek me with all your heart. And I will be found by you."

So how do you reach for your destiny right now? Maybe, you say, you've prayed and nothing seems to happen. You still aren't seeing your way, finding your purpose, realizing your dream.

TO HELP YOU MORE

God Is at Work in You—to Perfect You

In 2008, I was privileged to accompany Joel and Victoria, along with other family members, on a visit to meet Billy Graham at his home. Like you, like people all over the world, I had grown up watching the reach and depth of this great man's ministry.

Billy Graham had preached in person in more than 185 countries to more than 215 million people during seventy-plus years of ministry. By the time he was ninety years old, when we met with him, he had prayed with every American president from Harry S. Truman to George W. Bush. I'd seen his meetings with world leaders captured in news headlines and on television. I'd watched his crusade meetings fill football stadiums where people would rush forward after his talks to the song "Just As I Am," their hearts pricked in wanting to know and live more for God. He had been a great inspiration to our family as we watched him reaching people's hearts, one great message at a time.

So I was a little in awe standing with my family round him in his living room. Reverend Graham was not the young man I had seen on television, young and full of energy. But he was strong, gentle, and full of compassion. His once bold voice was soft and wavered now. I will never forget being in his presence. Before we left, my brother Paul and I asked Reverend Graham if he would sign our Bibles. In true Billy Graham style, the words he left for each of us were not his own, but the powerful, loud, and lasting words of God.

Philippians 1:6, he inscribed in a wavering hand in the front cover of my Bible. It was one of my favorite Scriptures, "For I am confident of this very thing, that he who began a good work in you will perfect it until the day of Christ Jesus."

He who began a good work in you will perfect it. How I believe those words! How I knew from many fears, disappointments, distractions, heartbreaks, and losses in my own life that God has a purpose and plan even when we don't see it.

The great God who gave Billy Graham a great purpose has a great purpose and plan in mind for you, too. Read Philippians for yourself today, and begin to search the Bible for what you would claim as a life verse, something that speaks just for you and to you about the desires and calling you sense from God.

Write this verse on an index card to carry with you or in your Bible, and think upon it daily. God's Word is God speaking directly to you. He has begun a good work in you and he will perfect it.

It's too easy to get stuck in disappointment or despair, in a rut of routine or by circumstances that allow our focus to turn away from what God would have for us. It's too easy to let someone else—bosses, friends, or family—say, "Don't expect too much from this life. Prepare for all that's bad. Prepare for nothing good to come from within or without."

Instead, we must consciously make the effort to pull from what we know in our gut to be true: that we are made for more, that God has something bigger and better in mind for us. That a life of drudgery and despair is not what he intended for his masterpiece. He intends us not to just survive in life but to thrive. That means, above all, you must think on these three things:

1. See yourself as a person of destiny

Change the way you think about yourself. Many times we project our insecurities on God. *He can't use little ol' me! What do I have to offer anyone?*

He says, *Put no confidence in the flesh.*[15] He means, *Don't trust in your own thinking or someone else's, or in your own power. Trust in me, Almighty God.*

Begin to see yourself in a different light. View your life as a gift that God has given you to fulfill. You have assignments that only you can fulfill on this earth.

He tells us, *You have been chosen and predestined according to my plan and purpose.*[16] *You are my workmanship, created in Christ Jesus to do good works, which I prepared in advance for you to do.*[17] When he created you, he did it right! You are the only you in the world! You are unique and fit for your destiny. When he formed you in your mother's womb and created you, he said, *It is good!*

2. Do something now to fulfill your destiny

What are you waiting for—the economy to get better? To win the lottery? To get a big break?

Maybe you need to make a move. If you do nothing, then you get no results. If you step out in faith, though, God goes with you—and in a powerful way.

An amazing story about four lepers shows us this.[18] Their city of Samaria had been taken captive by their enemies, and on top of that they were in a severe famine. Things were so bad that people lost all hope. But these four men decided to make a move. They decided to do something.

They could have resigned themselves to their circumstances and said, *Woe is us. We are sick. We are considered unclean. What could we possibly do about this situation?* Instead they determined, *Why should we sit here until we die? Let's do something lest we do nothing at all.*

They crept into the enemy's camp to get some food. To their amazement, no one was in the camp! The spoils were just...sitting there.

As these men were walking toward the camp, God was with them. God caused the enemy to hear what sounded like an army marching upon them. So when the encampment heard the sound of chariots and horses, they were seized with panic and fled for their lives. They left everything, which these four men from Samaria found. The foursome walked right into their enemy's city and began to eat the food and carry away the spoil.

Only the foursome was really a band of five. For their great victory was with God.

Had the four men done nothing, had they chosen to buy into all the negativity of the labels that other people put on them—LEPERS, UNCLEAN, UNWORTHY, UNTOUCHABLE—they would have died with the rest of the city. Instead, they reached out for their destiny. They believed God would be with them, and he was. They marched toward the enemy's camp, and God made the sound of their steps mighty. He scared away the enemy with each step of faith these men made.

So it is with us. You must do something, otherwise you do nothing. Why should you sit in defeat with everyone else when God has a destiny for you to fulfill? Tell yourself: "I have been in the famine too long. I have been in captivity too long. It's time for a march of faith!" When you move away from others' limits, God will move. If you make a move in faith and it's not the right move, God will show you. But keep doing something and watch what God will do.

What can you do today? You can:

- **Plan** for starting that business you always wanted. Every shop begins with an idea, and great companies are built one brick, board, or transaction at a time.

- **Pray** for your neighbors and coworkers. God hears. He's listening to you, the things you say aloud or silently in your mind, right now.
- **Find a way to use your gifts** to help someone in need.
- **Volunteer** in a ministry at church. (I can speak from experience, How we need you!)

3. Expect God to direct you daily

Get up every day and ask, "God, what do you have for me today?" Start listening for God's appointments and assignments. Look for the opportunities he has for you right now, right here, today. You will be surprised at what he will bring to you. Your great destiny is only a call away.

The Bible says, "Trust in the Lord with all your heart; do not depend on your own understanding. Seek his will in all you do, and he will show you which path to take."[19]

Do you see? Do you hear what God is telling you about your chapter, your destiny, your story in his book? Many times we are in such a hurry throughout our day that we don't even recognize the very opportunities God is placing before us:

A person in the grocery story who needs a smile.

A coworker who needs a word of encouragement.

A neighbor who needs a helping hand.

Your family, who needs some uninterrupted time with you.

Or, someone sent to encourage you and help you.

I was in the hair salon one day when a lady told me that she had enjoyed my teaching CD on fulfilling your destiny.

"Now that I have you in person," she asked, "tell me, what is my destiny?"

That was a loaded question! What surprised me even more was how I responded: "You are walking in it right now. If your trust is in God, he is directing your steps today."

It's true, though this idea took me a while to grasp. But not because it's complicated. Destiny is not an ethereal ideal that cannot be understood. It is simply allowing God to direct your steps daily, no matter what situation you may find yourself. It is knowing that God has a plan for your life that is bigger than you. It is trusting God to fulfill that plan as you daily look to and acknowledge him.

Get Ready to Live like God Meant

Each of us has those days when it's difficult to believe we're that masterpiece that God made, that we are a miracle in the making, that God has something great just ahead. Too often we feel like ordinary wall paint that's all one tone and not even covering well. But if you look and listen to your life, you'll find reminders of God's brushwork everywhere. He's using all the darkness and light, all that's faded and bright in your life to make you beautiful. He's performing little miracles every day to get you to the destiny that he designed from the beginning. You may not see that any more than you would see all the foundational work da Vinci did on the canvas of the *Mona Lisa* to give her that mysterious, beautiful smile. But then, God's reminders aren't always so subtle either.

I still run into some of the women who cared for me when I was a sickly baby. They love to remind me of the miracle God gave me, noting that when they would pick up the infant me, I was dead weight.

Destiny is not an ethereal ideal. It is allowing God to direct your steps daily, knowing that God has a plan for your life that is bigger than you, trusting God to fulfill that plan.

"Like a sack of potatoes," one woman is fond of saying.

But God had more in mind for me than to be dead weight. My parents determined to claim more of a destiny for me, too. They prayed for more, and isn't it amazing how the miracle needed was just a prayer away?

Yet how many times do we set out with some great expectation, only to receive frustrating news—maybe even devastating news—that stops us in our tracks. We believe in the best but get the worst. The job that helped you buy your house is no more, and without work you might now lose the house, too. The mobility we once enjoyed is gone because, by accident or disease, so is our health. The love we thought would last forever is suddenly lost.

I'm telling you: there's a choice to see such things as challenges or, as I like to see them, as preparation for great victories to come.

You can be devastated or determined.

You can believe you're a mess or a masterpiece.

You can choose to wait for the world's woe or God's graciousness.

God loves it when we're faithful to where he has placed us, when we refuse to give up, and when we ask big. He loves it when we say, "Okay, Lord, I'm having a tough time swallowing this. I don't know if I can bear, let alone lift, anymore, but I'm going to press on." He loves it when we say, "That person is discouraging me, this circumstance is telling me to go no further, that doctor is saying I won't have the ability, but I'm not going to be left behind on the destiny you have for me, Lord. I'm going with you, wherever you take me, however far I have to go. I want to not just step into what you have willed for my life. I want to walk in it. I want to run. I'm not giving up."

God loves it when we say, "I want to taste all the goodness you have prepared for me. I want to lift my head toward the heavens. I want to hear your desires for me and not just speak for you, God, but shout and sing."

You see, your destiny is precious to God. You may not have a strong memory for Scripture, but maybe you can lift boulders to build churches or lumber to create hospitals. You may not be able to sing, but maybe you can whisper blessings as you mop a schoolroom floor or cook a hamburger for a hungry restaurant customer.

You are his masterpiece and in his book. Your happy ending has God coming to rescue you on a white horse.[20] You have only to reach for God's hand and ask him to start telling you the story.

3
Finding More When People Fail You

Because You're Made to Be Loved

❧

I grew up in a godly home, full of love and peace. While my family was far from perfect, my parents were genuine, real people of integrity. Because of their love for one another and us and others, they served in full-time ministry all their lives. My mother is still the matriarch of the church, Lakewood, that my father founded with her when she was just twenty-six years old—and she still keeps us all straight! We are a close-knit family that enjoys time together and likes to laugh. Our parents taught us that. So we make corny jokes and do silly things together.

We all work in ministry, too. Paul, my oldest brother, is an associate pastor at Lakewood Church. He gave up his medical practice as a surgeon, and he and his wife, Jennifer, moved to Houston with their five children after our dad died. I am the next in line, serving as an associate pastor at Lakewood, and my husband, Kevin, serves as the COO. We have three wonderful children—Catherine, Caroline, and Christopher. Our middle sister, Tamara Graff, and her husband, Jim, pastor a thriving church in Victoria, Texas, and have four children. You probably know our brother Joel best, next in the lineup of Osteens as "the smiling preacher." He stepped up as pastor of Lakewood and has sold more than five million copies of just one of his encouraging books. And, yes, it's true, Joel's been smiling all his life. As a child he was somewhat shy, but he always had a big grin on his face and still does as he and Victoria serve Lakewood with their two children. April Simons, the youngest of us, will tell you that she is the favorite child (but of course, I know I am!). She and her husband, Gary, pastor a great church in Arlington, Texas, and have five children.

I have the greatest nieces and nephews!

So having grown up with siblings I love dearly and in a fun and godly home, I wanted to create the same for a husband and children of my own. In fact, if you would have asked me when I was young what I wanted in life, I would have responded without a beat, "To marry a minister and have five kids!" I loved growing up in the church, and I was excited to start my own family.

But our plans are not always the way things work out in this life.

Everybody Falls into a Pit Sometime

Things don't go like we wish. Dreams come crashing down on us. We can trip over what falls at our feet. We can fall. We make mistakes and fail others. Sometimes, you could say you dove into those fallen places. Other times you can fall into a pit unawares. Or you can be pushed. You can come from a great home, be an overachiever, and do all the right things motivated by only love and goodwill, and still you, too, can stumble, trip, or—worse—be dragged down.

The point is you can end up in a pit, just like Joseph in the Old Testament.[1] Joseph was a young man, just seventeen and excited about his dreams coming to pass. Yet his older brothers, full of anger and jealousy toward him, set out to destroy his life. They stole his prized coat, threw him into a pit, leaving him for dead. Fortunately, the eldest talked some sense into his brothers, and instead they chose not to kill him. But they still did something terrible. They left Joseph in that pit and sold him to the next passing caravan—their enemies—and into slavery.

Where was God in all of this chaos? Were Joseph's dreams a figment of his imagination? Was this his lot in life, to live a life of slavery rather than a life he had seen in his dreams?

I have found in life that just because others throw

you into the pit, or just because you fall into one, doesn't mean you have to live there! You are made for more than that.

Somehow Joseph knew that, too. Like Joseph, you too will face loss and hurt and wrong. There will be struggles. Things won't go like you expect. Deals will fall through. Promises will be broken. People will fail you.

I understand because I fell into a pit, too.

As a young woman, I dated very little. I did attend my high school prom at Humble High School with a guy from our church. Actually, I asked him out because I wanted to go with a nice boy. (I will never forget what I wore that night: a long, peach-colored, sleeveless gown with a matching hat. Before you say that might have been the beginning of my fall, I promise you, it was in style back then!) My date, Ronnie, looked so handsome in his white tuxedo. We went to dinner, then the prom itself, and I was back home by eleven!

Then in college, I enjoyed the company of friends in groups, girls and guys, and dated some, but no one that really interested me as the marrying type.

That is, no one until I met Tom (the name I will give him for the sake of this book). Tom was a guy in one of my classes but not just any guy. He was kind and a gentleman. His parents had founded a church in another state, and Tom wanted to follow in their footsteps. He was preparing to enter full-time ministry.

Perfect, I thought, charmed by who Tom was, who he said he wanted to be, and the life I imagined we could create together.

We dated for about one and a half years before we got married. We were both twenty-two years old, and I thought I had found the love of my life forever. Tom and I moved to his home state. We were both enthusiastic about helping his parents in the church, and I was so happy. God gave me the desires of my heart. He made my dream come true. A husband! A godly family! Ministry together!

But our plans don't always turn out the way we imagine. It wasn't very long into our marriage, only a year and a half, when Tom began to change. He laughed less. He became very solemn. He made unusual decisions. He thought I should leave my full-time position at the church and get a secular job. I didn't understand why, but he was adamant.

So I got a job at a nearby university, but this didn't seem to make Tom any happier. He seemed to become distant to me, cold, disconnected. When I look back, I think maybe he had a plan to distance me from his family, his work, our church, himself.

Then the nightmare began. He went on a two-week fast and at the end announced I needed to go back home to Houston for a while.

Stunned, I thought, *Tom, you need to eat something because you are not making any sense. You must be delirious from food deprivation!* He wouldn't budge. Then I asked him all the questions any woman would: Are you having an affair? Why are you doing this?

I got nothing, only that he denied an affair. Tom simply said, "Go home."

I was crushed. I thought I was home, our home that we were making. Finally, in desperation, I said, "Let's go talk to your parents."

Tom agreed.

I felt hope. I thought, *We've always gotten along with his parents. They will help figure out what is going on, they'll talk some sense into him.*

It's Dark Down There in the Pit of Heartbreak

Tom's parents, however, did not offer the helping hand I expected and needed. They didn't talk any sense into Tom at all. They said simply, "Let's pray together before you go home."

Really? For the second time that day I felt stunned, like I was in the Twilight Zone. My thoughts raced: *Didn't they see this situation was crazy? Didn't they know that Tom wasn't making any sense?* Confused and hurt, I got into the car, resigned to go home with this man who suddenly seemed a stranger. Tom drove in silence and then, back at our apartment, went away from me to another room.

I felt so alone. I needed to talk to someone who loved me. I called my parents. My mother and father were right there. My mother told me she loved me. My father listened to me cry. They both shared my shock that no one could change Tom's mind.

Finally, Daddy said: "Lisa, hold up your head high. Don't beg him to stay one more minute. Come home, and we will try to work out everything."

Though I wanted to stay up in the night and try to talk things out, Tom totally shut me out. Lying on the bed next to him I kept asking myself, *Who is this stranger?*

My parents gave me the strength the next morning to pack a suitcase and get in the car as Tom drove me to the airport. Little did I know that I was just beginning my journey into the pit. On that long drive, I wanted to believe Tom was coming back to his senses because he cried and I cried. He hugged me and told me that he loved me. I held on to that as hope that this horrible event would soon pass and we would be back together.

On the flight back to Houston, I sat in a window seat and cried the whole way, my face turned toward the window so no one could see my tears. My parents met me at the airport, comforting me as my father drove us home. But the facts were clear. I was twenty-four years old and going to sleep that night in my childhood bedroom. Only I was no longer a child. I was a young woman who had a taste of her dream, the desires of her heart, and they had all been shattered. Never did I expect this scenario. That first night in my old room seemed surreal. As my eyes danced around the room catching glimpses of high school photos, the dresser that my mother and I picked out together, I couldn't help but think I was dreaming.

TO HELP YOU MORE

The Seven Stages of Grief

After the first few weeks of returning home to Houston, I was overwhelmed with emotional pain like I'd never experienced. Thankfully, a guest speaker at our church shared seven stages of grief that people encounter after the death or the loss of a loved one. This helped me immensely to know I wasn't going crazy, but working through my emotional hurt. Based around the ideas of Dr. Elisabeth Kübler-Ross in her 1969 book, *On Death and Dying*, these stages will help you get through the pain and emerge stronger, more resilient, able to love and be loved again.

1. **Shock and Denial.** You react to the loss with numbed disbelief, maybe denying the reality of your loss in order to avoid the pain. This may last for weeks. But shock provides emotional protection from being overwhelmed all at once.

2. **Pain and Guilt.** Shock eventually gives way to emotional pain that may seem unbearable. Don't try to hide from it, avoid it, or escape with alcohol or drugs. You may feel guilt or remorse for things you did or didn't do, and life will seem chaotic and scary. But this is a phase that will pass. You will come through and find yourself wiser and more able, and your heart will be larger and stronger for what you endured.

3. **Anger and Bargaining.** As frustration gives way to anger, you may lash out and lay unwarranted blame for your loss on someone else. Feelings of wanting to fight back or get even with an ex-spouse; for death, anger at the deceased, blaming them for leaving. Attempting to make deals with a spouse who is

leaving. Begging, wishing, praying for them to come back.

4. **Depression, Reflection, and Loneliness.** Just when you think you should be getting on with your life, you may enter a period of sad reflection. This is normal. You may find yourself wanting to isolate yourself on purpose, to reflect upon things you did with your lost one and focus on memories of the past. Use this solitude and reflection to process your grief.

5. **The Upward Turn.** As you start to adjust to life without the one you loved, your life becomes a little calmer and more organized. Your physical symptoms lessen. Your depression begins to lift.

6. **Reconstruction and Working Through.** As you become more functional, your mind starts working again. You find yourself seeking realistic solutions to problems posed by life on your own. You start to work on practical and financial problems. You reconstruct yourself and your life without who or what you've lost.

7. **Acceptance and Hope.** During this last of

the seven stages of grief, you learn to accept and deal with reality, finding a way to move forward.

Of course, with God's grace and mercy, I believe, like me, you will defy the odds and come through with great victory and joy.

I swore my family to secrecy about it, saying: "This will work out. No one has to know I am home." I wanted to deny and hide from others what was happening as I tried to resurrect everything on my own. I was definitely in the first stage of loss and grief, which is shock and denial.

I began calling Tom, who refused to answer me. That didn't keep me from trying over and over again. It didn't stop me from asking my father to go with me on an unannounced trip to see Tom, either, a desperate attempt to resolve things.

When Tom and his family barely acknowledged us and refused to talk about the situation, I had my father take me back to the apartment I'd known only as a young wife. I packed a few clothes and returned to my childhood home broken, disillusioned, and full of rejection and shame. Not only had I failed in my marriage, but I felt as if I failed God and my parents.

Somehow, and I didn't even have a clue as to how, I'd failed Tom. I wanted to just stay on the floor in my room and not go anywhere or see anyone, I was so ashamed and grieving.

These were the darkest days of my life.

Everything was taking a toll on my body. For six weeks I stayed in the house. I kept losing weight, which, at just five feet four inches, I couldn't afford. I'd always struggled to keep my weight at ninety-five pounds most of my adult life. Suddenly I was at eighty-one pounds because I had no appetite.

I was so unsettled that I wanted to escape the present. When I went to bed, I wished it were morning. When I awoke, I wished it were bedtime. I was depressed and struggling with nonstop, negative, hopeless thoughts.

Where to Turn in the Pit

When you're deep in the pit of despair, what a gift it is for someone to hear you and love you right there. It's a gift for someone to reach out to you and remind you that you may have been hurt but you're not unable to heal. Your dreams may be broken, but they are not beyond rebuilding.

My father was such a gift to me. I spent many days crying, shut away in my room, and then my dad reminded me that I was not a worthless piece of trash that someone throws away. He reminded me that I am a valuable child of my Heavenly Father, God, who sees me as his treasure and has given everything for me.

"Lisa," he said finally, "you can't hide forever. You have to get out. You have to see your friends. You have to go to church again."

I knew he was right. Continuing to hunker down was only causing me to spiral deeper into depression. I didn't want to live in this horrible place of darkness. But I was afraid to let people know what was going on—that somehow I'd failed in my marriage. Even though I didn't know how I'd failed, the very fact that Tom didn't want me anymore made me feel like a failure. Add to that my feeling wounded and fragile. I thought how the slightest judgment from any of our friends would ruin me.

My father must have sensed my fear. He said something that forever will ring in my ears: "Lisa, we need to let the church know what you are going through so they can pray for you. People love our family, and they know we are real and have problems just like everybody else. We have always been honest with them."

My parents were not ashamed of me. They were not ashamed to ask for help and prayer.

Their love and their humility to receive love

showed me two of the most important first steps for getting out of the pit.

1. Look out for help to be unleashed

Reach out to friends, family, and people who love you. Don't isolate yourself from the very people who can help and encourage you.

I decided to trust my parents and trust God. I didn't feel like I could trust. Feelings had nothing to do with the decision. I had to choose it. In the pit, you're not going to be so trusting. But you can make the decision to trust. You can make a move to reach up and out. You have no idea how things will go, even if they will work out, but when you choose to reach toward God, who wants the very best for you, and see what he will do, I guarantee two things will happen: you will change or your circumstances will change.

I was about to see a little of both, but not like I expected. First, for me to reach out meant not just getting out of my room but going to our church, which then had a congregation of about four thousand people. I needed support. I felt awkward, embarrassed, ashamed.

So my daddy humbly asked the church to pray for me: "Our family needs prayer right now. Lisa is going through an unwanted divorce and she is hurting."

As he made the announcement, I cried, my parents

cried, and you could sense the compassion of the people around and behind us. Without any invitation, they came up to where I was sitting on the front row and began to hug me. They were so kind, and I was relieved that finally I didn't have to carry the burden alone.

I don't recommend that you announce your problems to the whole church, but it was right for me because it helped me move out of the denial stage and enter the healing process. For you, the best first step might be to tell your pastor or a counselor. Since our family had been in the spotlight during all the good times, it was right to bring this prayer request to the spotlight, too—and I can tell you it was freeing. It unleashed love not only within me but around me. The immediate love of people who crowded around me to pray for me and hug me was a balm. I knew I didn't have to go through this alone. I didn't have to fix things. I just needed to be faithful.

TO HELP YOU MORE

The Saving Power of Love

At sixteen, my friend Debra George was ready to end her life because of a broken relationship. Stung by her boyfriend's words when they broke up, Debra made a last-ditch attempt to convince

him to take her back. She called him from her
mother's kitchen, but once again, he rejected her
plea. Debra hung up the phone, feeling as broken as all her ex-boyfriend's promises.

She reached for dozens of pills, determined to
end her life.

But God wasn't ready for that. He had more
for Debra to do. She sensed an unusual, peaceful
presence that caused her to stop and reconsider.
A hope-filled thought came to her mind: *I can
make it without that person's love and affection. I
am going to be okay.*

She threw the pills down the drain, and to her
surprise was able to sleep peacefully that night.
Little did she know what she would find on the
other side of her pain.

God knew because he was waiting there all
the time. Debra started spending time with him.
She found his love was like no other: without
condition, merciful, tender. She knows now it
was God who brought her peace that night she
almost took her life.

Today, Debra speaks and writes about God's
great love, his power to save us when people fail
us—and people always will. (Her book, *When
Hurt Won't Stop: From Devastation to Destiny*,
tells more of her story.) She especially loves

working with young people who, like herself
once, didn't think they could go on with life because of a broken heart.

I have prayed with many people who have experienced suicidal thoughts and a darkness that
they describe as an intense pressure to give up
and kill themselves. Those thoughts are coming
from Satan, our enemy, who desires to steal your
life and destiny. I want to encourage you to
think on God's thoughts instead, because his
plan is to see you through any hardship and give
you a life of peace and joy.

You may not be able to see his plan right now,
but before you give up on yourself, I want to ask
you: What will happen if you push on through?
What is on the other side of your hopeless, discouraging thoughts? Could it be the relationship with someone you have always longed for?
An undiscovered gift you have to help others?

Are you dying for someone to love you like
you thought you loved them—with all your
heart?

Someone already has, you know. His name is
God, and he's waiting for you on the other side
of your pain.

2. *Look up for the love and grace of God to help you*

One of the most powerful truths when you're in the pit is you don't have to fix things. You can't always. There are things no human being can fix. For you it may be the death of a spouse or a child. Or, as for me, maybe the unfixable thing is a divorce. Or maybe it's a really bad breakup with those who were once your dearest friends. No, there are many things you can't fix. But you can be faithful through the agony. You can reach for God and his people. You can run to church, where you can be surrounded by prayer and people who also struggle and need God.

My father had always said, "The church is not a museum to display perfect people, but a hospital for the hurting."

He was right. In the hospital of church, healing can begin. For me, the act of confessing a need for help was like cleansing my wounds of fear and shame so I could begin to get better.

Now people were checking on me. With the love of God, for weeks after the announcement, they were encouraging me, reminding me that I was valuable and loved, and they were praying for me. Bit by small bit, they helped me think beyond my situation and myself.

I determined to go forward in my life. I started working at the church, and I began to dream again of ministry. It was refreshing to be out of my bedroom and getting back to a normal schedule. It was fun working with my sisters, April and Tamara…but Joel was a different story! He often left notes on my desk telling me I had been demoted or fired. Of course, he signed it, "Daddy!" (I told you we liked to joke around with each other, and some of us take it way too seriously!)

With nothing to hide in the darkness of my pit, I felt free to walk again along a path back to wholeness. The Sunday I confessed my need for prayer, I went home from church feeling stronger—and in the following weeks, as

My father had always said, "The church is not a museum to display perfect people, but a hospital for the hurting."

I went to church and served there, I went back stronger, too. This became a cycle. As I continued to reach out and look up to God for help, I found people who loved me and prayed for me. I was not alone in the pit, not meant to stay down there. Life hadn't turned out as I imagined, but God still had a plan for my life, and he was forging the road ahead of me.

Healing Heartbreak Takes Time

Healing, however, is a process, and the beginning of it doesn't mean you'll not still feel confused or hurt at times. You will. I was still heartbroken. I continued to hope Tom would change his mind. I continued to write him letters and ask how we could work out this separation. I continued to pray for reconciliation.

My letters and calls remained unanswered.

Three months after coming back to Houston, I received divorce papers at work. I guess deep down I expected them, but on the surface I'd been in denial, hoping divorce would never happen. I remember opening the large envelope, seeing the word *divorce*, and quickly shutting my office door. I let my body sink into my chair like my spirits. Those papers represented the death of my marriage and the death of a season in my life. Tom and I were young and had only been married two years. This seemed wrong on so many levels.

The love and prayers of our friends and church strengthened me, but there's no denying that the weeks and months following were tough. I still felt abandoned by my husband and my dreams. I still had no answers from Tom on why he wanted the divorce; as I searched my soul, I felt more confused and hurt. The stress and despair mounted, until I thought my nerves would explode.

Several times I called my dad at his office for encouragement and comfort. After all, I had to give my mother a break at home! One time, in a fit of tears, I said, "I am having a nervous breakdown! I don't think I can take it anymore!"

"Lisa," my father responded, ever-patient, ever-encouraging, "you are not having a nervous breakdown. You are going to be just fine."

"No," I insisted. "I am having a nervous breakdown right now!"

Oh, the joys of parenthood, right?

That is not how my father responded at all. He was kind and loving, patient—and he happened to be in a conference with our longtime friend, Dr. T. L. Osborn, with whom he shared my story.

TO HELP YOU MORE

How Will I Get Through the Hurt I Feel?

You may not feel God is listening at times. But he hears you. Lovingly, he is working out things for your benefit. Still, it is true to our nature to want to see that and feel that.

As a young lady with a broken heart, I remembered the words of God, "He heals the brokenhearted and binds up their wounds" (Psalms

147:3). I was that person who needed a real touch from a real God. I went with my good friend Kathleen on a short trip to New Orleans, to get away and pray. I petitioned God, "Help me. I want to go on with my life, but I can't go on with this heavy burden of rejection and hurt inside. Heal my broken heart."

Kathleen prayed for me and with me, too.

Nothing happened that night as we prayed in that New Orleans hotel room. There were no thunderbolts. There was no sudden change. I faced another dark night.

But when Kathleen and I got up the next morning to do a little sightseeing, I will never forget what happened. As we walked down the street, I felt a certain relief, as if God reached down and lifted a great burden off of me. The heaviness and oppression lifted. It was real and amazing.

That day God healed my broken heart.

The commercial says, "What happens in Vegas stays in Vegas." I like to say, "What happened in New Orleans stayed in New Orleans" because I left my broken heart there.

The truth is: God hears and God heals. He will work things in his time. Keep talking to him, keep believing, and he will show you that

> he is an anchor to be trusted. With him is the relationship of your dreams.

Dr. Osborn asked to talk with me.

"Lisa," Daddy said, "there is someone here who wants to encourage you."

How could I have known this was one of those divine appointments that only God could orchestrate?

Dr. Osborn was so kind. "Lisa," he said, "you know I love you like my own daughter. I want to talk to you like a father for just a moment. Is that okay with you?"

I agreed.

"Lisa, I know you are hurting and I am sorry for your loss. I want to ask you a question. Do you know why you are crying so much?" Without waiting for an answer, he said, "It's because you are feeling sorry for yourself."

This is encouragement?! I thought. I wanted to say, "Is there anyone else there I can talk to?" But I stopped crying for a moment because Dr. Osborn got my attention.

"I know what it is like to hurt because I have lost a loved one," he said.

I knew he knew. His only son had passed away at the age of thirty-three. I shifted.

"You are not the only person who has ever gone

through a divorce," he said. "Others have gone
through this, too, and they have recovered. I know
you are hurting, but it's time to dry your tears, hold
up your head high. Let God take the scars in your life
and turn them into stars for him."

How God Turns Scars into Stars

It's said the truth hurts, and, yes, sometimes it does.
The truth of Dr. Osborn's words seared my soul. But
as Dr. Osborn spoke to me from his own wounds, the
agony of losing his only beloved son, I heard important truths. I could hear those truths because he spoke
it with such love, great love—and that love is what
will get you through any heartbreak you have, too.
Here's how.

The truth that hurts also heals

The Bible encourages us to speak the truth in love and
states that wounds from a friend bring healing.[2] This
friend of our family knew what it was like to hurt,
and he loved me enough to lift me out of my pit of
self-pity. He knew that I was made for more than that
ugly mire of the pit.

Healing begins when self-pity ends

Dr. Osborn showed me that healing begins when self-pity ends. This was a major hurdle in my healing process, because up until this point I was stuck in the pit, in self-pity and depression, and Dr. Osborn's words helped catapult me out of my pit.

In fact, never again did I cry over Tom or my situation. I was grieved, yes. But I didn't cry. I didn't continue to torment myself with the *whys*: *Why did this happen to me? Why did Tom reject me? Why do I have to go through all this pain?* Sometimes we will never know why, but the most important thing is to take a step out of self-pity.

One thing that helped me was to focus on others instead of myself. One Christmas after my divorce, after having lunch with my family, I went to a mission in Houston and helped feed the homeless. Joining others who felt broken, even though broken in different ways, helped me as I offered help to them. The act of going to the brokenhearted and getting my focus off of myself made my world larger. I began to focus more on the people I met instead of my own troubles—and it's hard to feel sorry for yourself when you look into the troubles of others.

Allow God to turn your why? *into* wow!

Look what God can do when you simply put your trust in him. *Wow!* Look what he can do when you release control and allow him to dream a bigger dream for you. Dr. Osborn used his woundedness to minister to others, including me, and his great love erased my *whys*. He showed me that God had more ahead for me if I would look for it, reach for it, be willing to live above the pit. He helped me hear the truth and move forward instead of staying stuck in a pit of sadness and tears.

The Bible says, "No eye has seen, no ear has heard, and no mind has imagined what God has prepared for those who love him."[3]

There is so much truth in that. The things we think might destroy us, the people who fail us, the relationships broken, instead can enlarge our hearts.

Crawl out of the pit mentality

Joseph could have wallowed in self-pity and grieved his scrapes and scars from being thrown in the pit. But I like Joseph, because even though he was in a pit, he didn't let the pit get in him. He didn't develop pit mentality. That's when you think, *There's no hope for me in the pit. I'm stuck in the pit. My mama was in the pit and I will always be in the pit. I don't have anybody to get me out of the pit!* No, Joseph put his trust in

God, and by doing so all of his dreams came to pass![4]

So even though you've begun to climb out of the pit, and begun healing, how do you avoid the pit mentality?

I wondered this over and over. The thoughts that were swirling in my mind tossed me to and fro as if I were on the roller-coaster ride of the century and couldn't get off. Disney World's infamous scary ride Tower of Terror had nothing on me!

One of the prevailing thoughts I had was that I must have been a terrible wife for my ex-husband to shut me out of his life. I wracked my brain trying to figure out what went awry, what I had done wrong. My self-esteem was at an all-time low.

Even though I tried to move forward, there was a big part of me that felt I was disqualified from being in the ministry. I felt like I had the big D for *Divorce* now tattooed on my forehead. Ministers were supposed to be the example in this area. *What example could I be?* Worse, I thought I would never get over my sense of rejection, my broken heart. How could I help others when I couldn't help myself?

The only way I can explain it is that I felt there was a battle going on inside my head. One negative thought after another, every waking hour. All of a sudden I realized that I must take control of my thoughts before they took control of me. It almost seemed like an impossible task, but I decided to do it one thought at a time. That strategy made all the difference.

When a negative thought came to me, I made a deliberate choice to stop and deal with it immediately. First, I would say, "I choose not to dwell on that thought," even though everything in me wanted to go there. Then I had to replace that negative thought with one of God's powerful thoughts about me. This is the key. Begin to fill your mind with hopeful, positive thoughts from God's Word that you can meditate upon. When I thought I couldn't make it one more day, I would choose to dwell on these thoughts instead:

- I can do all things because Christ Jesus is strengthening me![5]
- I will make it because God's grace is sufficient for me today![6]
- God has a good and a bright future for me! I believe what he says about me![7]

When I said those words, I didn't feel like I had a bright future, but I chose to live by the truth instead of my emotions. Emotions are fickle, but God's Word remains true. As I chose to believe the truth of God's Word about me, I was defeating hopeless, negative lies one thought at a time.

This took an intentional choice, self-control—and it became a true battle, like hand-to-hand combat.

Negative "pit" thoughts would crop up, and I would strike back with a Scripture passage that brought encouragement.

Hope Replaces Heartbreak

As I continued to fight, I noticed that my life began to transform little by little. The negative thoughts were being drowned out by the powerful thoughts of God. My countenance began to change, and I started to smile again. I got my appetite back. I began to get stronger spiritually, physically, and emotionally.

The Bible says the person who trusts in the Lord will never be disappointed.[8] God's Word was coming true before my very eyes. My hope was returning, and not only did I notice it but others around me did, too.

I had come out of the pit. I was looking up. God delivered me into my destiny in a way I would never have imagined.

As I chose to believe God's Word about me, I was defeating hopeless, negative lies one thought at a time.

I often thought of Dr. Osborn and how he used his heartache to help others. I realized when you have been in a pit, you can help others out of their pit. Dr. Osborn did it for me, and I want to do it for you. Today, I want you to know that you do not have to stay in the pit. I made it out and you can, too. The pit is not what God made us for—he did not design us to live in the dark. Every night is followed by morning, and every valley is flanked by hilltops and mountain peaks.

I went through a divorce I still don't understand. Dr. Osborn lost a beloved son. Joseph was hated by his brothers and was sold into slavery. So many dreams are shattered or stolen for a while. But God restores them. He gave me a life and ministry beyond what I imagined. He helped Dr. Osborn love a world of people who loved him back. He brought Joseph to a place beyond his dreams.

On staff now at Lakewood for more than twenty-five years, I've seen God restore peoples' dreams every week. I've seen him take the scars in the lives of people and turn them into stars. To this day, I have never had true closure to my divorce. But I can tell you this: God has turned my *why?* into *wow!* He has restored old dreams and given me new ones. He has brought me out of the pit to a new place, where I can look up and look out, and like Dr. Osborn, like God, I don't see the scars.

I see *more.* I see stars.

4
Finding More
When You're Distracted

*Because You're Made to Reach Your
Destiny*

❧

After my divorce, I was so broken that all I could
see was my own need. All I felt was my own hurt.
During this extremely stressful time in my life, I had
become terribly anxious and tormented by depressing
thoughts. My body began to react to my mind and
my emotions. I felt drained and fatigued. I couldn't
eat and lost weight. I couldn't rest well. I was depleted
in every way, and this was unlike my typically optimistic, energetic self.

Tormented by my emotions and lack of energy, I
was having a tough time shaking the thoughts of rejection, hurt, and disappointment. These thoughts
distracted me at times from what was going on with
others. I was just so incredibly sad. The thing that I
had fought on my knees, the very thing I believed
would not happen was happening: a divorce. *This is
something that happens to other people,* I thought, *but*

surely not me. I kept somehow hoping that this was a bad dream that I would wake up from, but as sunrise turned into sunset each day, I was forced to face reality head-on. I was now among the ranks of the divorced.

Within weeks of the announcement, someone in the church came to me and said, "Lisa, I'm hurting, too. I'm going through a divorce. Will you pray for me?"

And then another person asked essentially the same thing. And another.

My first thought was: *Are you kidding? I need somebody to pray for* me. I didn't feel qualified, but I began to pray for each of these people and encourage them. *What is going on?* I wondered. *God, I need help. Can't you see that I am hurting?* Then, ever so gently, God began to orchestrate my steps in a way that I never would have expected. He began to help me focus on others instead of being stuck and focused on all my own hurt and pain.

I was turning a corner in my life—just like the eighteen-wheeler trucks I see on the Texas highways. Before they make a turn, the trucks must be slowed down. The driver must make sure there is enough room to maneuver, and then gradually the long truck can make the turn. Can you imagine what would happen if the driver of this vehicle attempted to turn without ever slowing down? The truck would tip! It would crash! There would certainly be a lot of damage and injury.

In the same way, God takes us through the turns of life gradually, slowly, so that we can adjust and be able to keep going forward.

In my newfound venture of praying for others, I began to give my time to them, too. I took them under my wings, loving them in their hurt and pain as I'd been loved in mine. I began to call and check on them. I understood the pain they felt. I knew the confusion and hurt. I could relate in so many ways.

I will never forget the night, soon after I began doing this, when several people literally pleaded with me to start a weekly meeting for those who were going through a divorce, separation, or marriage struggles. I wasn't sure if I was the right person to lead this, but I certainly wanted the prayer myself and for others in the same horrible circumstance.

So on Tuesday nights I began to lead a prayer group. Quickly, I felt more was needed. Within a few months, the group of about a dozen people grew to more than 150. I wanted to find tools and insights for everyone, like myself, grappling with divorce and its aftermath to use in moving forward with life. Then couples began attending, wanting help for their marriages. How could I also equip them to handle conflicts and challenges?

The idea of a class began to stir in me. *But I can't*

teach such a class, I reasoned. *Who would listen to me? I'm broken myself! I don't have the answers. I couldn't fix my own marriage. I'm no example.*

Are You Going to Look Away?

It's an awful thing when you think you're disqualified by your past or by present circumstances from doing the thing you desire and feel called to do.

Being called means you can answer!

So many things can get in the way, though, starting with ourselves. Do you see how quickly I disqualified myself from doing something good? How easily I was talking myself away from this desire to help others?

Thank goodness no one was hearing my inner thoughts. Thoughts like: *How can I give hope to others to move forward when I feel like I'm stuck in this horrible moment of time? How can I assure those around me that their pain will go away when I have lingering thoughts that my pain is here to stay? How can I dry someone else's tears when I feel that all the largest buckets in the world are unable to hold mine?*

A funny thing happened, though. As I thought of what disqualified me, I also thought of the people who needed hope just as I had. An unexplainable strength began to rise in me. I call this well of strength *grace.* Though I have heard and studied the definition of *grace*, which is "unmerited favor," this inner strength goes far beyond any dictionary's definition. This strength, this grace, was knowing that somehow, somewhere, someway, someday, I would come out of my own pain, and until then I must take the grace given me to help others out of their personal tragedies and brokenness. I began to think: *If I can just put someone else's heartache before my own, that goodness would surely come around to me again and fulfill me.*

Though I still struggled, thinking, *I'm not a public speaker or gifted minister,* down deep I began to venture on the precipice of believing: *Maybe this is what I'm meant to do—help out of my own place of trial.*

Then one day, from teetering on that precipice of belief-unbelief, I took the leap of faith. I decided to seize the opportunities staring me in the face. Doing what I had been doing—focusing on my own hurt—was getting me nowhere.

Do You See What More God Has for You?

Have you been there before? You want things to go one way, but God leads you another. Isn't that what our relationship with him is all about? You allow him to point you in the direction he has in focus for you. You become less distracted by your own needs. You stop being blinded by your own pain.

I began to find more when I started teaching the Word of God. Teaching wasn't easy. I agonized over every session. I studied and fretted as to whether or not I was preparing the right things, if I was presenting them in a clear and true way. I was so nervous speaking in front of everyone. But the people in my class didn't seem to notice or question me like I questioned myself. They were so hurting, so hungry for help, just as I had been in those first weeks after my divorce. They just wanted encouragement and to hear God's promises for more in their lives. They wanted to be reminded, as I had been reminded by my father and so many others, that they mattered and there was something more ahead for them.

The funny thing is that as one need came to me, I stumbled ahead to meet it in the best way I knew how. Soon, more and more needs came to my attention. With each need, I forged ahead, trying my best to help others. Before I knew it, I was teaching and preaching on a regular basis.

That was when my dad asked me to preach for him on a Sunday while he was away traveling. He knew I was up to the challenge, even if I didn't. Despite the limitation I put on myself, despite how I had for a time been distracted from helping others, he believed in me. My parents had always taught us, "See a need and fill it. Find a hurt and heal it."

Maybe this isn't so difficult after all, I began to think. *Maybe my own pain is what helps me to help others— they're more ready to listen to someone who has been where they are, who is still working through it all.*

Suddenly I saw so many hurts and needs around me. I hardly had time to think of my own hurt and disappointment. I remember looking up toward Heaven and saying, "Okay, God, what are you up to?"

He must have smiled. He knew I was beginning to catch the vision he had for me. I was beginning to not be so distracted by my own brokenness that I couldn't tell others of his healing hand. In the eyes of others, I could have rightfully sat down to do nothing during this time except spend my energy on figuring how my life could have taken such an unexpected turn.

That is the thing we miss when we get distracted by discouragement, or that false sense of worthlessness, from following our calling, the desire of our heart. God plants those desires and that calling in us.[1] He wants us to recognize it, see it, live it, and reach for more. It's so easy to let things distract us from fulfilling our calling, our destiny. For me, the temptation was to give in to naysaying and that false self-talk that I wasn't good enough, successful enough, to help others. There were other distractions, too.

For one (a big one), I was nervous to speak in front of others! Yes, I was so honored to preach for my dad. I was thrilled to be able to share God's Word, but I had a lot of fear. *Would I do a good job? Would people really listen to anything I had to say?*

Lakewood is such a big church. It's not unusual to have people from all over the world and all walks of life at our services. Yet I felt as if I was just now learning to teach a handful of people, a small group. When I got up to preach, anyone from drug dealers off the street or gang members from the inner city to political figures and well-known personalities would be listening. What did I know about drugs or gangs? The only drug I knew about growing up was when my siblings "drug" me across the yard, and the only gang I was ever in was the Bible Study gang at my church. And how could I be relevant to politicians and celebrities? They are so gifted, so eloquent in their speech.

Attractions versus Distractions

Have you been there, wanting to do something that you feel you were made to do, but then you stop yourself? There are so many distractions. Maybe you say, "I could never start that book group. I love to read, but I never studied literature. There are people more qualified than me." Or you tell yourself: "I would love to get a Saturday hiking group together, but others know these trails so much better than I do." Or you resign yourself, saying, "I could really help people figure out their tax returns with my experience in accounting, but why get bogged down with that now?"

A hundred little things can stop us in our tracks from seeing and following the goodness God has paved for us. We get blinded by our own disqualifications. We fail to see our own destiny.

You can wake up morning after morning, thinking, *Another day has passed and nothing's happened in my life.* Or you can start turning around those negative thoughts and begin to see all God has in store for you. The choice is yours: remain distracted from your destiny or grab onto it, because for every distraction there are attractions toward that purpose you're meant to live. Just as flipping a switch brings light, there are things that can propel you toward living with more fulfillment and purpose, with more effect on those around you. There are things you can do and think upon to pull you toward your destiny. Instead of thinking of your life as miserable, start seeing your future as bright. See yourself doing everything God means for you to do. Keep that vision in your heart and in the forefront of your mind. That is what vision is all about. That is how attraction works—you focus upon it and think on it. Take a look at six of the major attractions.

1. Vision versus blindsightedness

You've probably heard the proverb, "Where there is no vision, the people perish."[2] Isn't it true? Without a dream in your heart, a desire for or a sense of calling to something, you can feel so unfulfilled. You miss so much.

We can be blindsighted to how God can use every bit of who we are, even our failings or our wounds. But the mother who always wanted children and then sees her adopted kids laughing as she tends to them finds joy. The mechanic who's missing a finger but always wanted to fix things can feel good when he repairs that Chevy's broken fan belt. The administrative assistant who works from home and always loved to organize knows satisfaction when she smooths out a schedule knotted with conflicting appointments. These are ways people have found what God designed for them to do. That mom could have lamented not being able to bear children naturally. The mechanic could bemoan his maimed hand. The administrative assistant could complain she's not in the office with everyone else and can't know what's on the docket for everyone's day. But each of these people found ways to act upon their vision for their life, to reach the destiny God had in mind for them. They are doing the thing they were meant to do—in spite of what might have stopped them.

What is that thing for you? Is there some desire you've let lie dormant? Do you know for sure? Are you waiting for a glimpse? What are you focusing upon? Are you looking at what you have or don't have, what you can do or can't do? Maybe you've been distracted by disqualifying and negative thoughts.

"Now is not the time for me to pursue this." *But if not now, when?*

"Someone else can do this better than me." *So why are you the one with the desire and not someone else?*

"I know this is needed, but what if it probably isn't wanted?" *How can others want what isn't offered yet? How can a need be met if no one ever tries?*

TO HELP YOU MORE

Let a Word (or Two) Work for You

During one of the most stressful times in my life, I decided to fight against the pressure with words—God's Words. I sat down and wrote on a piece of paper all the Scriptures I could find about how God gives us his strength and joy and peace even in the midst of trials. Promises like:

The joy of the Lord is my strength.

God will keep me in perfect peace as I keep my mind fixed on him.

I am strong in the Lord and his mighty power.

God has a great future for me.

I didn't feel like saying those things. In the state I was in, I was struggling to believe them. But I believed words have power, my words— and that God was watching over his Word to perform his promises. I took God at his promise, too (in Jeremiah 1:12), that what didn't seem to be making a difference before my eyes could change everything in the spiritual realm. I knew from enough examples in my life, and the lives of people in the Bible, that you can't live by what you feel. You have to live by what you know to be true. What is true is that you can be an overcomer instead of being overcome.

As I meditated upon those words I'd printed out and read and recited to myself, over time I began to feel relief, comfort, renewal. The stress eased. My anxious thoughts melted, a little at a time. My worries of "what if" turned to "because God." For example, instead of thinking, *What if I never get better?* I began to think, *I am already better because God is strong when I am weak.*

The disciple Luke wrote, "The Word of God grew mightily and prevailed" (Acts 19:20). I saw that in my own life. I found to be true what 2 Corinthians 10:4 says: that we can fight negative thoughts and events with even a word.

You can do the same. Maybe you start with just these promises I've listed above. But don't stop there. Search the Bible for additional promises of God. Look for the ones that speak specifically to you concerning your finances, marriage, health, or whatever area you need encouragement in.

Write down the promises that speak to you. Read and recite them to yourself. Keep them on index cards in your purse or pocket. Meditate upon what they mean. Memorize your favorites. Speak these good words into your life and share them with others.

Now watch what God will do.

I think about Babe Ruth, the famous baseball player who struck out 1,330 times, then went on to hit 714 home runs. It was reported that on one occasion when he came to the plate, he pointed his bat in the direction of where his next home run ball would land. He changed what he saw in himself. He looked away from a strike-out mentality and toward being a home run visionary. For thirty-nine years, his home run record remained number one.

You may feel like your life is filled with a lot of strikeouts. But what would the home runs look like for you? Do you have that picture in your mind?

That's a vision of what you can be—and what God can begin showing you when you begin to focus on what he has, what he can do, instead of all the limits you or others have placed on yourself. The Bible talks about stirring up the gift that is in you.[3] Remember how I began to feel a stirring toward helping others? It began with a simple step, a choice, a decision: A hope that God could use me, that maybe I could make a difference.

You can take that simple step right now, make a simple choice: Expect God's favor, wisdom, and direction in your life. Choose to believe that God means what he says when he promises to work things for your benefit and your good.[4] Believe that he has a plan for you—because he does. He has things in store for our future—not for calamity, but for good. He promises to restore our fortunes and our very lives.[5]

But how do you know what God is saying to you about your future? Where do you find your destiny? Besides the stirrings you feel, how can you know? God gives us guidance in the Bible. He tells us to write down the vision he gives for our lives, to make it plain on tablets so we can read it over again and run with it.[6] *The vision is for an appointed time,* he says, *and even if it takes time to come about, wait for it because it will surely become real.*[7] Take a closer look at how this works:

- **Search for it in God's Word.** Jesus showed us one way. When he walked on earth, he may have sensed his destiny and purpose, but how did he know for sure? He lived on this earth thirty years before he entered his ministry. Did it take him a while to form the vision for his purpose and life? The Bible tells us that one day Jesus walked into the synagogue and opened up the Scroll of Isaiah, a book we now have in the Old Testament, and found the place in Scripture where it was written about him.[8] Then he declared, "The Spirit of the Lord is upon me because he has anointed me to preach the Good News to the poor."[9] Jesus found what God's Word said about him. You can find words in God's book about your destiny, too. Are you searching for them? Do you read to see what God is saying about you? He will show you if you read his Word.

- **Run with it once you see it.** Once you see that vision God has for you, believe it and begin to run with it. Jesus did that, too. He began to preach and teach and help the poor in mind, body, and spirit— healing and performing miracles. He ran with what God had in store. He put the vision into practice. He believed it and expected it to happen.

- **Write it down.** You might be thinking, *Yes, but he was God's Son.* Did you forget you are God's child, too? Just as God had a great destiny in mind for Jesus, he has a great plan in mind for you. Keep your focus on him. Write down what you sense stirring in you, the Scripture you feel speaks to your life and vision. This has worked for the ages, going back to Bible times. "Write the vision down and…run with it."[10]

What is it you want to do? I was called to help others out of my own need for help. Are you called to learn and complete college so you can teach others and help them get an education? Do you have a desire to start your own business? Have you thought about sending some warm blankets to children in underprivileged areas? Could you, as my dear friend Irene does for our family, volunteer your time as a hairstylist to bless others?

Set your focus on your goal and on God. Expect him to make a way for you. Feed your vision with his Word. Find his promise for you and run with it.

2. *Confidence versus doubt*

No matter how clear the vision, anyone can get distracted from their destiny by doubts. Negative what-ifs can sneak in, like a little breeze that grows into a storm. God reminds us that doubts will toss us about like a wave on the sea blown and tossed by the wind.[11] You'll wash out that way, too, if you let the doubts take hold. Your vision will end up beached.

But if you ask God for confidence and to help you live out your dreams, your vision, he promises to help you.

Lay down any limits blocking your way, and God will lift up a way for you. Don't put your limits and lack of faith on God. He believes in you. He is a God of no limits. Why do we doubt his power and his ability? That's exactly what we do when we list our excuses and reasons why "it," whatever that is, can't be done.

The Bible is filled with stories of people who let their doubts get in the way of their destiny. Even though God brought the Israelites out of slavery, and performed great feat after feat to deliver

What if the people stopped questioning, asking, "Can God...?" and instead said, "God can!"

them from a cruel king, they doubted he could provide for them. God had parted the Red Sea for the Israelites to cross to safety. Once on the other side, they began to doubt.

"Can God take care of us in the desert?" they moaned. "Can he give us food in the wilderness?"[12] You know what God did? A miracle! He sent breakfast...and lunch and dinner and snacks in between. Every day, he provided manna—not just any kind of bread, but true Wonder Bread, bread from Heaven— for the people to eat.

What if the people had stopped questioning, asking, "Can God…?" and instead said, "God can!"

Can God get me out of the mess I'm in? God can!

Can God ever get me out of this insurmountable debt? God can!

Can God cause my trouble-filled mind to be at peace? God can!

Can God still believe in me though everyone else has given up on me? God can!

God will get you to your destiny when you focus on him and take confidence in him. Confidence begins when you expect more from God. This is what faith is: You stop looking at what's happening in your circumstances, and start looking at what God can do. You start claiming all the examples God's given us of his power, examples recorded in the Bible.

We're told faith comes by hearing the Word of God.[13] The more you hear God's promises and examples of his love for us and providence and mercy— and meditate upon this—the stronger your faith will grow. You will drive away doubt with what you know and what you believe. You will find confidence in the God who can and stop asking "Can God…?" so much. The beauty of this is you don't have to figure out all the steps it's going to take to get you to your destiny. You won't have to come up with all the answers. Your confidence in God lets him work out both the big things (those Red Seas) and the small (what's for breakfast).

3. Good words versus negative talk

What if you could change things with one word? In a way, you can. You can be your own worst enemy by the words you let slip past your lips, or you can tap into God's power with positive, truthful words. For example, remember all that negative self-talk I gave myself before starting the prayer group? What if I'd voiced those thoughts aloud, and someone heard them and believed them? The group, and then our class, and my calling of delivering good news, might never have gotten off the ground. Remember that many times we are our own worst critics. We have to learn not to be so hard on ourselves or beat ourselves up with our negative words and thoughts. But good words, both spoken and written on our hearts, make a positive difference.

Jesus said whatever we say and pray for shall be, and by our own words we will be justified or condemned.[14] Ouch!

If you speak negative, defeated words, you will have a negative, defeated life. But if you constantly speak words of belief and confidence in God's promises for you, then you can live as the overcomer you were meant to be. It's like the proverb says: "He who guards his lips, guards his life."[15] When you guard your words, you guard your destiny. When you speak God's promises, you release faith and even every good possibility into the atmosphere.

Several years ago, Kevin and I bought a home that was larger than our previous home. We were excited about having the extra space, since our family was growing, but we lacked furniture to fill several rooms and areas. For example, in our old house we had given away our dining room table in order to make that room our home schoolroom. But in our new home, it just so happened that when you walked in the front door, the first room you saw was the empty dining room.

We knew that in time we could buy a dining room table, but our budget didn't allow for it just yet.

Meanwhile, several friends reminded me how empty our house looked, and this sort of lit a fire under me. I did want a dining room table for our friends and family to gather round. So I decided to pray for God to help us furnish our home sooner rather than later. I found several Scripture verses and began to talk about them instead of the emptiness of our house.

Every day when I walked through our empty dining room I would say, "Father, you promised in Proverbs 24:4 that you would fill our home with rare and beautiful treasures. I thank you for providing the furniture we need for every room in this house that you've blessed us with."

A few weeks later, a couple knocked on our front door. Patty and Perry have been longtime friends, and I thought they just stopped by to see our new home.

"Merry Christmas!" they said. "We brought you something."

Instead of the small housewarming gift I imagined, they pointed to a truck. Our friends heard we needed a dining room table and hauled over their large, beautiful table. As they set the table in our dining room, they told how they'd decided to buy a more contemporary table for themselves and give their traditional one to us. The table was in impeccable condition and wasn't just any discard piece of furniture. It was as if I had specifically ordered it myself—a pedestal table with inlaid wood and finely carved edges. Completing the set were Chippendale chairs that were not only gorgeous, but had a fabric on the seat perfectly matching our décor.

God truly does honor his Word. I could have complained about our lack of furniture, but I knew that complaining would not change anything. And Patty and Perry's gift was just the beginning.

My sister April gave us some furniture soon after, and our empty rooms suddenly began to fill up with just what we needed—and more than we imagined possible just months earlier.

God, however, is not limited by our budgets—and he puts his Word on it.[16] I could have gone around saying things like, "My house is so empty. How are we ever going to get the money for nice furniture? I am so tired of waking up to empty rooms." But I believed God even cares about making a house a home, so the outcome was determined by what I said and what I believed.

Whatever need you have, remember God is faithful to his Word. Negative words can distract you from your destiny, but if you get your words in agreement with God's you will see him unfold his plans for you.

In the most trying times of life, it is vital to speak positive words, for your words are propellers that will thrust you out of where you are to where you wish to go.

4. Following God versus doing it your own way

If anything can distract us from our destiny, it's disobedience and choosing to follow our own ideas instead of God's.

The Bible is filled with stories of people just like us who chose badly. Samson's story is particularly striking to me. Samson was so full of promise—destined to save his people. But Samson went his own way. He chose to disobey the ways God set out for him.

God had given Samson a tremendous gift: strength like no other man on earth. For example, when Samson met a lion in the vineyards, he tore the lion apart with his bare hands. God's plan was for Samson to use that strength to be a great deliverer for the people of Israel.[17] Instead, Samson went without care into enemy lands, worshipped their gods, and insisted on marrying exactly the woman God hadn't planned for him. Samson's compromise cost him that remarkable strength—and his life. Because Samson insisted on his own plan, sadly, his wife betrayed him and allowed her people to capture and imprison him. While Samson did accomplish some great things for God, his life could have been better and different.

I have found in my own life that it always pays to follow God and his ways because he knows exactly what I need. God designed us for our destiny and has the plan laid out for us, if we will decide to follow him. He knows what is best for us, his children.

I love what my dad used to say: "After serving God all these years, the greatest thing I have learned is that God is smarter than I am!"

That may sound funny, but the truth is that sometimes we act like we are smarter than God by insisting on doing things our own way. The Bible says that God's ways are higher than ours.[18] He wants to lead us on the best path for our life.

Jesus said, "If a person really loves me, he will keep my Word and obey my teaching."[19] The words of Mary, the mother of Jesus, forever resound in my ears. She was speaking to the disciples about Jesus and said, "Whatever he tells you to do, do it."[20] How simple but profound. If we will but learn to trust God's ways and timing in our lives, and do whatever he tells us to do in his Word and in our personal lives, we will be greatly rewarded. Obedience truly brings blessings and rewards that no person could ever match.

Jesus promises, "I will guide you on the best pathway for your life and I will lead you and guide you."[21]

5. Gratefulness versus jealousy

If anything gets our focus off our destiny and distracts us from experiencing all God has planned for us, it's keeping our eyes on someone else. Think of all the people in the Bible who allowed jealousy to cut them off from the blessing of God. The Bible's chock-full of these folks, and things always go badly for them.

In the very beginning, in that first family, Cain gets jealous of Abel's offering and ends up killing his brother.[22] The first king, Saul, becomes jealous of David's popularity and winning ways and loses his position and, because he becomes consumed with jealousy, eventually his life.[23] Many times jealousy is the fear of being replaced by someone. No one can ever replace you because no one can be you. You are fearfully, uniquely, and wonderfully made and put together. If you feel you have been replaced on your job, change your thinking to be grateful about a better job awaiting you. After a divorce, if you're feeling like you're replaceable, then plant seeds of hope in your heart for someone greater who appreciates your value and may be around the corner.

Are you starting to see the picture? Jealousy, rivalry, and comparison, for that matter, will hold you back and keep you from God's best. Jealously will distract you with other things, too, because it always leads to unrest, disharmony, rebellion, and selfish ambition.[24]

Ambition in itself isn't bad. Ambition can help propel you toward what you're meant to do. But at the expense of others, selfish ambition keeps you from doing what God encourages: rejoicing with those who rejoice, being glad when others are blessed.

After all, we're not in a competition. We're on the same team. What God does for others, he'll do for you. We're all meant to do a good thing. Be grateful for that in others, and you'll find it within yourself, too. When you choose to be glad for the success of other people, you'll find there are others out there glad for you.

6. Patience versus impatience

What's the old saying—"Timing is everything"? It is! Imagine if you gave a twelve-year-old boy a Ferrari. He might have some fun for a moment, but he could do a lot of damage to himself and others from behind the wheel.

In the same way, if anything can derail us from our destiny it's trying to rush ourselves and God. If faith is anything, it is believing that God has a plan and a place for us in it, and he will unfold things as needed. God tells us we inherit his promises through faith and patience.[25] Sometimes we forget about the patience part. We get impatient! We want to see everything happen right away. But God is teaching us and equipping us to handle the great things he has in store by each little thing at a time. We must trust in his perfect timing for our lives.

I would never have been ready to teach a class for 150 people before getting my feet wet in leading a dozen people in prayer first. A young man can't get a license to drive before he's mature enough to handle the responsibility of a car and the rules of the road.

It's the same way with God. In the Bible, Moses had a passion to deliver the people of Israel long before he was prepared for it. He acted emotionally as a young man, and missed God. It wasn't his season yet. So God kept him in a training place for a few more years.

It wasn't until Moses was seasoned that God put him in place to lead the people of Israel out of captivity.

In my own life, God once impressed this upon my heart: *Lisa, silence does not mean that I am not working on your behalf.* After my divorce it looked like everyone around me was either dating or married. While my friends were seemingly out having a great time with their boyfriends or husbands on the weekends, I was studying for my next message to teach or preach. I couldn't help but wonder, *God, what about me? When am I going to meet someone?*

Proverbs 19:11 says, "A man's wisdom gives him patience." Wisdom says, *I'm not going to get off course. I'm not going to grumble and complain because it's*

Silence does not mean God isn't at work on your behalf.

not happening when I want it to happen. I'm going to keep my focus on God and the things of God.

You'll know when it's your season because things will start happening, like doors opening to you. If you are striving and struggling, trying to force things to happen, it's probably time to step back and practice patience.

Remind yourself: this is God's timing in your life. He has a plan. He knows what's best, even when you don't see it or feel it. He tells us he is always working behind the scenes on our behalf—we just have to wait for it sometimes.[26] In due time, he brings us right to the place he means us to be, the place where we can do and be what he designed from the very beginning.

From Distraction to Due Time

When I finished my first sermon at Lakewood, I knew I wanted to spend my life delivering God's good news. I knew God had prepared me for it one prayer group meeting and marriage class at a time.

Isn't it amazing how God desires to use us even when we don't feel qualified? Even after we've been distracted by negative self-talk by a lack of vision, by following our own ways instead of God's ways, by jealousies or other things? What if I would have listened to my own disqualifications for leading that first prayer group instead of the needs of others?

God tells us to comfort those with the comfort we've received.[27] I'm so glad I listened to him instead of myself.

You can do the same.

My dad used to frequently recite an Edwin Markham poem: "Ah, great it is to believe the dream as we stand in youth by the starry stream; But a greater thing is to fight life's battles through, and say at the end, the dream is true!"

I see the richness of that idea now. God has more in mind for us than the things that distract us in our youth or pain or discouragement. He lovingly grows and prepares us and brings us to the place where we can do what only we were designed to do in this world. The very things pressing on you now may be the very things he's leading you into blazing a trail for. You may be disqualifying yourself, but that is just a distraction.

Keep your eyes on him and he will show you the way. When you look back, you will see how God was leading you to make not only your dream, but his come true.

5

Finding More
When You're Heartbroken

Because You're Made to Live Your Dreams

∞

After my divorce, I suffered from a broken heart—
and a broken dream. I still longed to be married. I still
dreamed of a partner in every way: a husband, someone with whom to start a family and work with in
making a difference in this world. But for six years I
remained single, thinking my dream was over. I felt
like someone had ripped out my heart and stomped
all over it. Every now and then the pain might tempo-
rarily fade, but an ache remained. I had never experienced such hurt.

Do you know what I'm talking about? Have you
had your heart broken, your dream destroyed? Maybe
you've lost a person you loved or a job or your dream
home. Maybe the dream you had tucked away in your
heart has never come to pass. Maybe it's your hope
that's shattered.

Is life really just a series of relinquishments, lost
hopes, withered dreams?

What if I told you no—that it's not over till God says it's over? What if you could know for sure that dreams do come true?

Would you believe?

Would you live differently?

The Funny Thing about Dreams

Right after my divorce, I didn't date because I never met anyone who interested me. I had great guy friends. I stayed busy working at the church and traveling abroad to speak. I felt like I was growing spiritually and personally.

Deep down, though, my dream lingered. It seemed in limbo, like it might never come to pass.

I thought my options were slim. I politely turned down several guys who expressed an interest in me. More than once, I said, "There's no one I would even think about dating, especially in the church." I was certain that there had to be some great Christian guys in the church, but I was hesitant to go there again, to try dating after being so hurt by someone who I thought shared my same spiritual outlook and bond.

That turned out to be a good thing for me. I might not have thought that at the time, but after a divorce, you're hurting and vulnerable. That's not the best state to be in when looking for another relationship.

What is best is to step back. Breathe! Let God and time bring the healing and restoration that you need. Use your seasons of aloneness to draw close to God. You don't want to make a wrong choice during your time of vulnerability.

It was in 1989, that a friend introduced me to this tall, dark, handsome guy. Only I didn't think of him for myself. My friend had been interested in Kevin, who attended church services on a regular basis, always sitting at the back. She wanted a dating relationship with him. But Kevin was interested in only a friendship with her. So when my friend introduced us, my first impression was that he seemed like a great guy, warm and friendly, always nicely dressed. But that was as far as I let myself think on him.

Then my mother told me how Kevin volunteered to help members of our church with repairs in their home. That did it. That was all I needed to hear. Not only was Kevin good-looking, but he was kind and giving. I went on a mission.

First, I asked him if he would like to volunteer to help with security for our sanctuary. We definitely needed his help, but this meant I would get to see him on a regular basis, since I was the staff member assigned to meet with all of our security team.

Next, I made the move. I fixed him up with my baby sister, April.

See, I thought Kevin was younger than me. Since

April is eight years younger than I am, I thought he would be perfect for her. I've always been like a second mom to her, or so she claims. (She told our mother once that as a girl she really did think I was her mom! Our mother still laughs about that, and says, "Really! Who do you think prepared your meals and washed your clothes all those years?") So it's true: I've always been looking out for my baby sister. At that time, she was graduating from college and moving back to Houston to become our youth pastor. So I told her all about Kevin, and April said she looked forward to meeting him.

They dated twice.

At a local youth event, April met a young man who swept her off her feet. "Lisa," she told me, "I want to date Gary and I am going to let Kevin know." She paused. "You know, Kevin is a great guy. You keep trying to fix him up with someone else, but the truth is you like him yourself!"

April was right. I did like Kevin, and I had found out he is only six months younger than me—not that it really mattered! But I was hesitant to admit my feelings after being so hurt by the divorce. Kevin was actually interested in me, too, but he was hesitant to ask me out after I had played matchmaker with him and April. So we were sort of stuck.

My dad solved the problem. He liked Kevin greatly and was impressed with his character. One day after church, Daddy nudged Kevin on the arm and said, "You know, I have another daughter!"

That was all Kevin needed to hear. He asked me to go with him to an Astros baseball game on our first date. The game finished late that night, and we had a hard time finding a restaurant still open. When we finally did find a place, only the bar was still serving. But neither Kevin nor I drink alcohol.

The forces did not seem to be with us. But our date wasn't over! There were no other customers in the bar, so we decided to stay and order soft drinks and an appetizer. Kevin jokes that I was the cheapest date ever. He thinks that's funny.

So that was July 3, 1989. By that October 17, Kevin kissed me for the first time. On Valentine's Day, 1990, he told me he loved me. On July 3, 1990, he asked me to marry him.

But who's keeping track?

There's a Dream Keeper

Do you see how God restored my dream? Even when my original dream went wrong, he worked (and he had to!) to still bring me the desire of my heart. When I least expected it (I was looking out for my sister!), when it didn't seem possible (my dad had to intervene!), when the timing seemed a little strange (there wasn't a restaurant where we could dine and linger and talk!), God worked things out in a beautiful way. He did that for me and he longs to do that for you.

Do you believe that?

Dreams require that, you know: belief in them, faith in them. A dream from God requires faith because dreams don't come to pass overnight. Mine took six years. Dreams require faith because we can't accomplish them without God's help—he sometimes has to enlist friends, sisters, and dads.

Of course we don't always see that, not any more than I could see, at first, that Kevin was perfect for me and not my friend, nor my sister. But whether we realize it or not, God is at work right now, today, in our lives. He's making things happen that we don't even realize—yet. See, *yet* is the key, because if there's one thing we can count on, it's that when God begins something, he will complete it. That's his promise.[1] In fact, the Bible tells us, God wants to not only complete things for us, but bring our lives to a flourishing finish.

I love that word: *flourish.* God doesn't mean to just finish the job on each of us. He means to finish with a flourish, grow us luxuriantly, have us thrive and prosper and achieve success.

That means no matter what's happening in your life right now, no matter what you've lost or what dream has died, it's not over. You may be going through a difficult time, but God promises to take care of the things that concern

God is at work right now in our lives, and when he begins something he will complete it with a flourishing finish.

you. He wants to bring you to a flourishing, thriving, abundant finish.[2]

Why do we sometimes struggle so much with believing that?

You Reach Your Dreams by Rocky Roads

The struggle's as old as time and maybe because of the very nature of realizing a dream. The path is never easy, never smooth. There are sure to be dark places, dips and pits. Remember Joseph in the Old Testament, whose brothers stole his coat, threw him into a pit to die, then sold him into slavery?[3] Joseph's dreams were what got him there. His brothers had even taken to calling him a dreamer and were jealous of his dreams and that beautiful coat their father gave his favorite son.

Like us, when a dream seems over before it's even begun, Joseph could have just seen the darkness of the pit. He could have believed his hopes had been forsaken. But, just as for us, God had more in mind.

Of course Joseph could no more see that than we can in those dark, lonely, sad pits of our lives. He was sold into slavery and could have given up on his hopes, his dreams. But something kept him going. Something made him refuse to give up on his dreams.

It wasn't the worth someone else put on him. Joseph's brothers had sold him into slavery for only eight ounces of silver. They didn't put much value on Joseph. But somehow Joseph knew God valued him. Somehow, with nothing else to count on, Joseph counted on God finding him precious when no one else did.

It was probably a struggle to believe on those long, hard days of serving as a slave. But Joseph chose to believe God cared and had a plan for his life. You might feel enslaved by a circumstance right now, but you have that choice, too, the choice to believe God cares. God sees. God is working things out for that grand, flourishing finish he has in store.

For Joseph, that belief was beginning to come into the focus of reality. The road from the pit Joseph had been in was leading to a palace, for it just so happened that one of the masters he worked for was a man named Potiphar.[4]

Now Potiphar was one of the high-ranking officials for the ruler pharaoh, and Potiphar genuinely liked Joseph. In fact, he turned over all of his affairs for Joseph to manage, not only his work but his whole household.

Do you think that was coincidence?

No, when God's hand is upon you, he will cause you to be noticed wherever you are.

TO HELP YOU MORE

Find Your Heart's True Desire

One of the most valuable lessons I learned after my divorce was that true fulfillment can never be in one person. I felt like I could not live without my ex-husband because he was my world at that time. Even before marrying Kevin, whom I love with all my heart, I realized one person cannot be my whole world.

People will always disappoint you. They will hurt you or let you down, even when they've taken a vow to love you forever, even whether there is a divorce or not. I know people who are single and desperate to get married. I also know people who are married and wish they were not.

There is only one being with the ability to

meet all of your needs, and that is God. Are you on intimate terms with him? How much time do you spend with him? How deeply do you know him?

After I went through a divorce, I began to spend more time with God and experienced my Heavenly Father as never before. I thought I knew him—his love and care, his presence in my life. But as I shifted my priorities from looking to people as my source of strength to depending on God for everything, I saw how little I'd known. During my times with him I began to see how personal God really is. When I reached out to him during my darkest season, he not only reached back, but he picked me up and carried me through.

I began to see God is the only anchor for the great voyage into the seas where life will take us. No matter where we are, or what relationship we are in, he must become our anchor because relationships and circumstances can shake us and threaten to sink us from time to time.

I often think about the story in John, chapter 4, about the woman at the well that Jesus met on his trip to Samaria. She had gone through five marriages and was working on man number six when she met Jesus. She tried to fill the void in her life with relationships, only to fail again and again.

After she encountered Jesus, however, she left his presence a different person. She declared, "Come see the Man that is the Christ" (John 4:28–29). This woman experienced the only man who could truly fill the missing void in her life.

When you find yourself lonely, you must know that you are never alone. Morning, noon, and night, God and the Son and the Holy Spirit are available to you. There were many nights I lay awake in bed wishing it were morning. But when morning came, I wished it were night again. I wanted to hide in bed and not face the day. I learned in those days to talk to God 24/7, and he was always there for me.

I encourage you to pursue God with all your heart. Begin with prayer. Talk to him. Plan times and spaces in your day to do this:

- Do you like to take walks? Make them prayer walks. With each step, give God your cares. This will take you to a place of peace and comfort.
- Do you give yourself a break in your busyness?

Take time during your day to express your love and thankfulness to God. He will refresh you like no other time-out.

- Do you sometimes find yourself stuffing worries about situations as they come? Every time a worry enters your mind, tell God your private fears. Talk to him silently from your heart, as you would a dear friend. He is your friend who sticks closer than a brother. The Bible tells us he wants to be your best friend (Proverbs 18:24, John 15:15).

- Do you need a coffee break to face the day? I love to drink my Folger's coffee in the morning with God as I talk to him and read his Word. I feel as if we are old friends spending time together.

You may not feel God is listening at times. But he hears you. Lovingly, he is working out things for your benefit.

Joseph could have struggled with still being a slave, still being upset that his dreams hadn't come to pass. Instead, he focused on God. Joseph made that choice, and he did an excellent job. That didn't mean things were easy and went smoothly, though. There were challenges. He had to manage all of Potiphar's affairs, but he couldn't manage Potiphar's wife. She was a doozy—or, better put, a floozy. You see, Joseph was handsome and well built, and she was attracted to him and set on seducing him.

Joseph, choosing again to keep focused on God and do the right thing, stayed away from her. One day, though, she attempted to entice him, so he turned to run out of the room and she snatched his coat.

Poor Joseph. Always losing his coat. Potiphar's wife took Joseph's coat to her husband. She told Potiphar that Joseph tried to attack her. Of course, Potiphar was furious.

Once again, Joseph was cast away—this time, to prison.

The guy couldn't seem to win. Even when he tried to do the right thing, he ended up sunk in a bad place. His dreams couldn't seem to ever come true. He could have given up on them. The road from the pit was not so easy, not smooth at all. That's where Joseph can teach us something.

Just because the road is rough doesn't mean things are over for you

When Joseph was thrown in prison, things weren't over for him any more than when he'd been thrown into a pit. God hadn't forgotten Joseph any more than he's forgotten you when it seems you only get persecuted for trying to do the right thing and live the right way. God's at work even when you don't see it. You may feel forgotten, but God never forgets about you.

Once, when I was going through a difficult situation and it seemed like God was on vacation. I asked him, "God, what is going on? It seems like nothing is happening."

God impressed upon me: *Lisa, silence does not mean that I am not working. People may shut a door in your face, but I will open another door.*

When things look their worst, you can dream again

Opening another door is exactly what God did for Joseph. He opened a door to the palace. Joseph kept dreaming his dreams, and he kept serving faithfully, steadily, until the jail warden trusted Joseph enough to put him in charge of the whole prison. It was in prison where Joseph met the pharaoh's baker and cupbearer. These men had gotten into some trouble, were imprisoned, and while there had some baffling dreams.[5]

No better place for a dreamer. Joseph interpreted their dreams and they came to pass exactly how he said. The baker soon after was put to death, but the cupbearer was restored to his position. Joseph pleaded with the cupbearer, "Please remember me to Pharoah because I have been unjustly accused." However, the cupbearer forgot all about Joseph, who sat in that prison for two more long years.

So Much for Dreams, Right?

Wrong. Joseph's hopes and dreams weren't over. God was at work. God hadn't forgotten Joseph. Neither, it turns out, had the cupbearer. After two years, he was in Pharoah's presence when his ruler was troubled by a baffling dream.

Oh yeah, the cupbearer remembered, *there was this dreamer in prison who could interpret dreams...* The cupbearer told Pharoah, who summoned Joseph.[6]

That very day Joseph left prison, never to return. He interpreted Pharoah's dream about a famine coming upon Egypt. Choose a leader to prepare the city, Joseph advised.

Pharaoh looked straight at Joseph. "You're the man," he said. "I choose you. Since God has made this known to you, there is no one as wise and discerning as you."

Was Joseph dreaming? One moment he was in prison and the next moment he was second in command. Do you see how God works?

Joseph was placed in charge of Pharoah's palace,

and all of Egypt submitted to him. That meant even Joseph's brothers and father, who were eventually led to the palace to ask for help during the famine. There they found Joseph, who had been in the pits more than once, and more than once had his dreams, like his coat, snatched from him.

Only now Joseph was wearing a linen robe. He had Pharaoh's signet ring on his finger as a symbol of his authority. God had not only given Joseph his dreams, but he delivered them in a way not even Joseph could have imagined: in a palace, with authority and confidence, royalty and restoration.

God loves to make dreams come true

What he did for Joseph, God longs to do for you. He wants you to know today: *You may be in a dark place, a pit, but it's not over. People you've loved may have forsaken you. Those you don't even know well may falsely accuse you. People you've helped may forget you. But I haven't. I never forget you. I will never forsake you.*[7] He longs only to raise you and restore you. He made you to hold on to your dreams. He knows life may take the coat off your back. You may face financial ruin. People may look to put you down, and you may feel enslaved to circumstances. But God waits to place a ring of authority on your finger. He's got your back and a finer coat waiting for you.

Doing right helps God get you to your palace

If you will trust God in the pit and in the prison, God will bring you into the palace. He will bless and favor you. The key to Joseph's turnaround in life is something we can easily overlook—the fact that he continued to do what was right whenever he was being wronged.

Have you been there before? How many times have you wanted to give back a "wrong for a wrong" response? Nothing good can ever come out of this mentality. But look what happened when Joseph chose to move forward with integrity: God rewarded him.

You may not be able to see it now, but the same God who did these things for Joseph will do them for you. He will restore the things taken from you. The Bible says, "God redeems your life from the pit and crowns you with love and compassion."[8]

Eight Truths about Dreams

Because God longs to crown you and causes you to reign in life in spite of what you go through, keep dreaming. Keep hoping. While you do so, prepare for God to go to work on your behalf.

1. Your dream has an appointed time

Timing is everything. The Bible tells us in due season we will reap, if we do not faint.[9] Understanding this fact will keep you from trying to bring your dream to pass yourself. Embracing this will keep you from missing God. Our dreams may not come to pass as quickly as we'd like, but God's timing brings his favor and divine connections.

Even this book has been a dream of mine for more than twelve years. I remember when God put the desire in my heart and I began to write down some ideas and thoughts for what I wanted to say. I have journals that document these notes and how I have prayed over this book.

There were a couple times over the years that I wanted to begin writing the book, yet just didn't feel that the timing was right. One of those times, I sensed God telling me: *Not yet. Not now. There's one more chapter to be written.* So I waited because I knew my dream had an appointed time.

Last year, I sensed the timing was right and began to pursue a publisher. All of a sudden, things began to fall into place. There was favor and there were divine connections. God's timing is always better, and sometimes it's sooner and sometimes it's later. It just pays to wait on God.

I didn't want to write a book just to write a book,

which was why I waited on God's timing. I wanted to write a book that would transform your life and encourage you to reach your destiny.

2. Keep the dream alive in your heart

Meditate upon it. Pray about it. Write it down. Eighty percent of Americans say they don't have goals. Sixteen percent do have goals but don't write them down. Less than 4 percent write down their goals. It is proven that goals are more likely to be reached when they are written down. So which group do you fall into? What would change if today you would write down your dreams and goals and bring them to God in prayer?

Ask God to prepare you and train you. Don't share your dreams with just anyone, but feed your dream in your heart. Just as Joseph kept his dream alive for years, your time will come; your cupbearer will present himself. Until then, keep your dream.

3. Your dream will go through a process

Joseph could look back on his life and see that God was directing his steps all along. For thirteen years, he walked in his destiny, even though he didn't realize it at the time. God was watching over him and positioning him for the throne. For six years, I didn't know God was preparing Kevin for me and me for him.

Know that like Joseph, like myself, you may not be able to see it right now but you, too, are walking in your destiny. Don't quit in the middle of the process. Don't give up in prison when the palace is right next door. History has shown that people who hold on to their dream for more than five years will see it come to pass.[10]

A friend of mine, Cerece, seemed to experience one hardship after another. Her well-known, affluent mother died suddenly and unexpectedly, which devastated Cerece but also took her into a five-year grueling court battle over her estate. You see, her mother was the companion of the late J. Howard Marshall II, an oil tycoon, who later married Anna Nicole Smith. You can imagine the media coverage of the trial that compounded Cerece's nightmare. If that wasn't difficult enough, her marriage ended in divorce and she raised three children all alone. But Cerece turned to God for help, and she kept doing the right things when it seemed all the wrong things were happening. She kept going to church, praying, and trusting God to get her through her trial.

Today, Cerece is thriving, not just surviving. She has three of the greatest children and serves the less fortunate people in the inner city.

No matter what life throws your way, fight for your dreams, even if it means losing your coat like Joseph and Cerece to keep your honor for what is your destiny.

4. The dreams God gives will always come with adversity

This will enable you to keep moving forward with boldness and tenacity because there are sure to be times you will want to give up. You'll encounter people who don't want to see your dreams come to pass. Persecution and opposition will come. Recognize it for what it is and keep doing the right thing. Keep a grateful attitude. Keep trusting God's goodness. Keep going forward because God's plan for you doesn't change when opposition comes. He's still at work, and he's not done. His work in getting you to the palace isn't over.

When in the pit, it's always important to keep a picture of the palace in the forefront of your mind. What is your palace? A new home? Your own business? Don't just name it. Think about it. Keep it in your mind's eye.

TO HELP YOU MORE

God's Got His Word on Helping the Brokenhearted

When my heart was broken, when the storms

of life threatened to sink me, the Bible became an anchor that kept me stable. I found stories of people like Joseph in Genesis, chapter 37, that encouraged my soul. I heard God's promises.

When I was just a young girl, my parents gave me a Bible in a translation I could easily understand. They taught my brothers and sisters and me that we should underline Scriptures and take notes as we read. "Don't be afraid to write in your Bible," they encouraged. "God will speak to you as you read it."

We learned that the Bible wasn't meant to be just a decoration for the coffee table, or so complicated and obtuse that it couldn't be read and understood.

The Bible is likened to a lantern that guides our steps. Psalm 19 says the Word of God revives our soul, gives joy to our hearts, and imparts understanding. When you read God's Word, it will transform your thinking and your life in a positive, hopeful way. I encourage you to take time every day to let God speak into your life by reading your Bible. I recommend you purchase a Bible version that is easy to read and understand, like the New International Version or the New Living Translation.

- **Start reading one chapter a day** in the Gospel of John about the life of Jesus. I enjoy reading one chapter of Proverbs and the Psalms each day because they are filled with promise and comfort.
- **Keep paper and a pen handy to write down your thoughts** about the chapter or any word of encouragement that you want to remember and meditate upon throughout your day. This tangible act can help lift God's promises from the page and make them memorable to you.
- **Don't be afraid to mark or highlight a Scripture** that speaks to you. Your Bible is not a revered relic but a treasured friend that speaks back to you. Your notations will not only chronicle your own spiritual journey over time but serve as a legacy of how God led you with his promises and his Word.

The Bible, I learned, was God speaking to me to encourage and empower me for every day. Just as we feed our bodies every day, I learned we must feed our spirit daily in order to be strong in all areas of our life. I encourage you to allow God to speak into your life every day through his Word.

Some people will compare you to the magnitude of the dream and they just won't see how it can come to pass. They will say, "Who do you think you are?" These critics may be your own relatives. Joseph's brothers were jealous of his dreams, but the fact is they ended up benefiting from his dreams. When God gives a person a dream, you may benefit from them, too—and not just you, but those around you. Don't let others' doubts discourage you, and be careful not to criticize your friends and family because of their own big dreams. God is at work for every one of us. He wants good to come from each of our dreams.

5. *When a dream is from God, it is so big that it takes him to make it happen*

Big dreams require divine intervention from God. When our father passed away in 1999, we didn't know what would become of Lakewood Church. Our father had helped found the congregation with our mother, and it seemed he was central to the ministry. But God knew what would happen. God had a plan.

My brother Joel, who had preached only the week before, felt a call to step up as pastor of the church. That in itself was a miracle. Joel had always worked behind the scenes in television production. Never before had he desired to be in front of people, even though my dad asked him to preach many times.

Of course his choice thrilled us, both our nuclear family and church family—and the church began to grow in magnificent proportions. Our small thinking of maintaining the church had suddenly changed as God gave us favor. We outgrew our eight-thousand-seat sanctuary and began to look for land or a larger facility, because we were landlocked at that site.

Someone mentioned to Joel that the former Rockets basketball arena, the Compaq Center, was available. This was a premier facility on a major freeway just a few minutes from downtown Houston. But how could we possibly afford this sixteen-thousand-seat facility? Joel called our longtime friend, then Mayor Lee Brown, who agreed that it would be a perfect fit for Houston and Lakewood. The price was not hundreds of millions as we expected, but only $12.3 million.

Our dreams began to get bigger, but were they too big for us?

We were not alone in wanting to purchase this facility. We were up against one of the largest developers in the nation. God can make anything happen, though. After three years, God graciously moved on our behalf and today we meet in this beautiful arena-turned-sanctuary, a place that has even become known as one of Houston's landmarks.

Could we have accomplished this on our own? No.

Joel and Victoria put their faith in God to bring the dream to pass. Our congregation prayed unceasingly. And without the divine connections and favor of God, our church home would have remained just a dream.

6. A dream from God doesn't make you look big—it makes God look big[11]

Lakewood's sanctuary stands as a monument to the goodness of God. What is impossible with man is possible with God. I encourage you to take the word *impossible* out of your vocabulary. With God, all things are possible. He is greater than anything you may be up against today. Like Joel and Victoria, expect God to do what you cannot do. And remember to give him the honor and thanks for bringing your dreams to pass.

7. A dream is from God when you try to let go of it, but it won't let go of you[12]

After my divorce, I tried to tell myself that I wasn't capable of standing in front of others to speak about God's love. I felt so inadequate, so beat down. However no matter how many times I tried to cast this dream aside, the thought that I could make a difference kept welling up inside of me. I couldn't shake it. It was my destiny. Whatever your dream is in life, you just can't shake it, because it's your destiny.

8. The power of a dream from God lasts longer than your life

God used Joseph to save Egypt and his own family, and many years later this very family line produced Jesus—the Messiah, our Lord and Savior. You don't know how far-reaching your dreams will be. God wants you to influence generations to come.

My dad dreamed big dreams—and the power of his dreams are still alive today. They live on through our family, through this church, and through every person he touched while he was on this earth. That's the power of a dream from God—so hold on to your dreams!

The Lover of Desires and Dreams

Remember how I said that there was no one whom I would possibly be interested in, especially at the church? How wrong I was. How comical we must look in the eyes of God at times. All along, Kevin was there and God had a plan.

Scripture declares God's plans are higher than ours, and his thoughts are wiser.[13] God's plans for us are for good and not evil, to give us a hope and a future.[14] Whether we see it or not, God's at work. He promises to direct our steps and to daily load us with benefits.[15]

God had been directing my and Kevin's steps for a long time. You see, Kevin grew up on a farm in Atlantic, Iowa. He and his twin sister, Karen, were the youngest of ten children. As a teen, Kevin had adamantly said, "One thing I would never do is live in Texas!" But when he was a young man, he was offered a job in Houston. He moved to Texas and his then girlfriend encouraged him to attend Lakewood Church. She and her family had watched my father on television for years in Iowa.

TO HELP YOU MORE

A Smile Will Get You Through

When you're heartbroken, few things can change your mood like a smile—both the one you get and the one you give. Whether you receive a smile or flash one, you'll feel better. And there's a reason for that. The Bible says laughter is good medicine for you (Proverbs 17:22), and a smile is part of laughter. There are real physical benefits, too:

- **Smiling makes you feel happier.** You can actually change your mood when you smile. The very act, when genuine, will have an effect on you. Try it right now. It's tough to frown on the inside when you're smiling on the outside.
- **You can give a smile when you have nothing, and get something.** Most people will smile back at you when you give them one of your smiles. Doesn't it feel good to be the catalyst of something good, something positive?
- **Smiling improves your face value.** Smiling actually makes you more attractive, and smile lines are more beautiful than frown lines as you age! You actually lift your chin and eyes and face when you smile, making you more beautiful.
- **Just as laughter is medicine for the soul, smiling relieves your body of stress.** You actually produce endorphins when you laugh, and when you smile you do something positive, releasing worries and fears. When you get those endorphins going you actually build immunities, too, as you're relaxed and your blood pressure lowers—so there are multiple health benefits.

SOURCE: Inspired by "Top 10 Reasons to Smile" by Mark Stibich, PhD, About.com (February 04, 2010); longevity.about.com/od/life-longbeauty/tp/smiling.htm.

Isn't that just like God? When I thought there were no candidates for marriage, and Kevin thought he would never live in Texas, God had a plan. When Joseph's brothers left him for a life of slavery and Joseph thought he'd be in prison forever, God had a plan—and a palace, and Joseph's back.

God's plans for us unfold at the proper time. We don't want to match wits with God. We see so little. We are limited in our thinking, but God is a God of no limits. There is a proverb to encourage us: "Trust God from the bottom of your heart. Don't try to figure out everything on your own. Listen for God's voice in everything you do, everywhere you go; He's the one who will keep you on track."[16]

I am eternally grateful that God handpicked my husband for me, and I am amazed at how God worked behind the scenes all those years on our behalf. He chose a farm boy one thousand miles away, used a girlfriend to get him to Lakewood Church, and brought us together, in spite of me trying to play matchmaker. My father performed our wedding, and my two sisters, Tamara and April, were my attendants. Kevin not only moved to Texas, but he married a Texan.

Who could have orchestrated such things but God? How could we know how beautifully he would make our dreams, the desires of our hearts, come true?

For beautiful it has been. When Kevin proposed, we were on Lake Lucerne in Switzerland; I had been speaking at different churches in Switzerland, England, and Bulgaria. Walking beside the lake before one of my talks, Kevin stopped me, looked me in the eyes and said, "Lisa, I love you and I am asking you to marry me." It was so romantic, and one year exactly after our first date.

But the desire of my heart wasn't just met with that marriage proposal. It was met with more tenderness than I could have imagined. Kevin said, "Lisa, I don't want to marry a person I can just live with—I want to marry someone I can't live without, and I can't live without you."

Four months later, when I walked down the aisle to take my husband's hand, a Neil Diamond song played during the ceremony. "The Story of My Life" has a line that remains a favorite of mine today: "The story of my life begins and ends with you."

The story for your life is in good hands. God, the maker and keeper of dreams, holds your deepest desires with tender care. Do you believe it? This is a choice. He is at work whether you believe it or not, whether you see it or not.

Talk to him. Pour out your heart to him, even your broken heart. He will keep the pieces. He will cradle your dreams, and in due time, when you are ready, when he has set everything just right and in place, he will hand them all back to you, restored, more beautiful, stronger than you ever could have imagined.

6
Finding More When You're Afraid
Because You're Made to Live Boldly

〰️

How do you go back to the place where something terrible happened? How do you look your fears in the face and move forward with your life?

As I mentioned earlier, after the mail bomb explosion, these questions got hold of me. I knew God was with me during that terrible event. I believed in his bigger plan for the rest of my life. I didn't have a doubt that he protected me when that bomb exploded in my lap. I knew he carried me over the days and weeks that followed: through the media storm, surgery, and into six weeks of recovery at home.

Why, then, was I having so much trouble with fear and anxiety there?

In the hospital, I felt so secure. Family and friends surrounded me throughout the day, often at night. Staff constantly checked in or was a call button away. Guards stood by my door, making sure of my safety.

I didn't have those things back home in the condo

I shared with my younger sister, April. I was so grateful for April and that I didn't have to be alone. But April wasn't the only one with me. Fear was there, too. Fear nudged itself into my everyday thoughts. Fear became that uninvited guest, a constant companion. Fear does that. It goes where it's not wanted and stays when it's not welcome.

For me, fear walked in when I thought how investigators never found leads to the mail bomber. Even today, all anyone knows is that the package was sent from a small town in North Carolina. Of course I wondered who would do such a thing. Immediately afterward, I began to think about some unknown person out there, somewhere, who tried to hurt our family. *Who was that person? Why would they want to do that? Would they try again?*

So when I went home, fear began to speak these questions, and more, louder and louder. Going in and out of the house, I'd think, *Someone may try to shoot me through the door or a window.* Or getting in the car, I became anxious: *There may be a bomb underneath.*

Fear kept trying to get my attention, and for a time I couldn't help but listen.

Fear Traps You

You know what I'm talking about—we all have fears. Most of us fear:

- bad news: *Will I ever recover?*
- rejection: *Why don't they love me?*
- failure: *Why did this go so badly?*
- making decisions: *What if I'm wrong?*
- trying something new: *What if I fail?*
- facing the unknown: *I have no idea how things will turn out.*

Others fear:

- their past being known: *Now people will dislike me.*
- what the future may hold: *Things could get worse.*

Maybe you have a fear of germs or sinking into deep waters, or your kids fear the dark. Some people fear being trapped in small spaces, like an elevator or a closet.

That's exactly what fear can do, after all. Fear pulls us down, traps us, paralyzes us, sinks us into inaction. We can get stuck in fear.

I got stuck by my fears after the mail bomb explosion. I didn't want to go out for fear that the bomber was still out there, or that another bomb might be waiting. But I feared staying home alone like a sitting duck, too, because the bomber might find me and strike me. I was stuck between going out or staying in, moving forward with my life or not budging from where I was. There were times that I just wished April and I could rent a bunch of movies, eat popcorn for days, and forget the mail bomb explosion ever happened.

It didn't take too many days of this before I realized that in-between place, that stuck place, is nowhere worth living. Down deep inside I knew that eventually I would have to conquer my fears. Was I going to allow fear to torment me and keep me from going forward? Or was I going to trust God to continue to take care of me as he had graciously shown even through a horrible ordeal?

I thought about another time I experienced great fear. Many years ago, my brother Joel, my sister Tamara, and I were on a small plane together. We got caught in a storm. I had never been in such turbulence. The plane rocked and shook, making us sick to our stomachs. We became scared. There weren't many people on the plane, but several people were throwing up, and everyone was visibly terrified. We all wondered the same thing: *Are we going down? Are we going to make it safely to the ground, let alone home?* Well, we did make it safely home.

Only, afterward, I did not want to fly again. I was

grounded until I resisted my fear to get on a plane and go. I knew that I could not do the things I dreamed of doing unless I conquered that fear. I did not want fear to steal from me, so I made the decision that I would continue to fly no matter how I felt. The first several flights were not comfortable, to say the least. I couldn't wait until we landed. But as I acted against fear instead of allowing fear to control me, I got comfortable. Now I have no anxiety in flying.

We're made for so much more than sitting around in fear. We're made to live boldly. That's why faith is called a walk. It takes us to the places God wants us to go, places he made for us, where he promises:[1]

I will help you.

I will hold you up.

I will keep you in my possession with my victorious right hand.

Five Ways Fear Works

To grasp God's victorious right hand, though, we must first get a grip on how fear works. Five facts about fear gave me that grasp:

1. Fear begins with a thought

Fear enters with just one idea, one feeling. Sometimes

that feeling can make you shake in your boots, as we put it in Texas. So what we do with those thoughts make all the difference in the world.

Whatever we think on repeatedly becomes a part of us. I'm sure you've heard the proverb, "As he thinks in his heart, so is he."[2] It's so true. If you allow them, fearful thoughts will control how you act.

In fact, psychologists tell us studies show that our lives move in the direction of our strongest, most predominant thoughts.[3] This makes perfect sense. If you're always thinking on the welfare of animals, chances are you spend a good deal of your vocation or volunteer or recreational time helping animals. If you are thinking about cars all the time, you either work in a field related to automotives or spend your spare time in something related.

When we think on something long enough, chances are we will end up acting out our thoughts. This is another reason why it's so important to guard our minds, choosing carefully which thoughts we accept or reject. Some people believe that we can't help or change the way we think, but that simply is not true. We can replace negative thoughts with God's Word and change the course of our life and destiny. The Bible teaches us: "Let God transform you into a new person by changing the way you think. Then you will learn to know God's will for you, which is good and pleasing and perfect."[4] If I would have continued to meditate on the fear I'd had on that turbulent flight, I would have never stepped back on a plane again. We must recognize when fearful thoughts come and nip them in the bud.

TO HELP YOU MORE

Fight Fear with Fear's Fight

Fear is aggressive, so you have to deal with it aggressively. Fear takes no prisoners. It will bear down on you to destroy you. Period. With such an enemy, you have to fight in the same way. Once you recognize anxious thoughts, feelings of being scared, immediately deal with them. Don't even open the door to it. Resist each and every thought of fear that comes to your mind.

Does that sound simplistic?

Maybe. But it's no more simplistic than fear's tactic of entering your mind and taking up residence, refusing to leave…until you tell it to do so. Where we get into trouble is when we begin to entertain thoughts of fear. We allow them to niggle at us. We start dwelling on them, instead of resisting them.

You have to choose not to give into fearful thoughts. The Bible shows us that we must be aggressive in pulling down and casting down any negative thoughts and strongholds (2 Corinthians 10:3–5). If someone handed you a snake, would you simply take it? No, you would absolutely refuse it!

You have to be just as adamant with fear. Refuse fear and you will experience God's perfect peace.

2. Fear torments your mind

Yes, that's right. Fear will bully you into chaos with discouragement, anxiety, and unrest. You will notice that fear always paints the worst picture in your mind, a picture of hopelessness and defeat. It will torment you with thoughts that harass and hover over you with the vague feeling that bad things are going to happen:

Your child is going to get on drugs.
You're going to get sick.
You're going to die young.
You're going to fail.
Nobody likes you.
You'll never be loved.
If you get on an airplane again, it's going to crash.

Fearful, tormenting thoughts are totally opposed to everything in God's character and Word. God's very nature is love, and perfect love casts out fear.[5] Instead,

God is saying to us *Fear not. Be strong and coura-geous because I am with you.*[6] We have to realize that God would never give us fearful thoughts, so we must refuse them. We must learn to trust God more than we trust thoughts of fear.

There is an interesting Scripture that shows us this. "All the days of the de-sponding and afflicted are made evil [by anx-ious thoughts and forebodings], but he who has a glad heart has a continual feast [regardless of circum-stances].[7] Fear brings anxious, foreboding thoughts of coming doom or misfortune. But God wants us to be glad of heart, joyful, and expectant.

> *We must learn to trust God more than we trust thoughts of fear.*

Don't allow foreboding, desponding thoughts to creep into your mind. Instead, picture good things happening to you, because God is a good God and he has a bright future for you. Think on things like:

Something good is going to happen to me.[8]
Goodness and mercy are following me.[9]
Angels surround me.[10]
God is holding my hand.[11]
Jesus is my Great Shepherd.[12]
The Holy Spirit is helping me.[13]

3. Fear is the opposite of faith

In fact, fear comes to steal your faith. Fear brings chaos, but faith gives you peace. Where fear wants you to believe in the negative, faith helps you know the positive. Fear is always connected with negative and bad things. Fear makes you nervous. It makes you shake and worry and shrink back—just the opposite of what God wants you to do. Where life would give you chaos and calamity, God promises calm. Where fear causes you to go backward, faith enables you to go forward. Where fear almost always tells you to run, hide, stop, or give up, faith keeps you going and fuels progress and success. Choose faith over fear.

4. Fear breeds bad company

Think about it. Would you worry if you weren't afraid? Fear doesn't come to harm you alone. Fear brings companions, and they are a bad crowd. Worry and anxiety come hand in hand with fear, and they will surround you with two more bad friends: doubt and unbelief. Who needs that?

5. Either you will control fear or fear will control you

There is really no gray area in the matter of fear. We have to ask ourselves: *Do I want to be controlled by fear or by God's peace?* Fear is very aggressive, so you must be aggressive in resisting it and acting against it. You cannot be passive and expect it to go away on its own.

Fear becomes a problem only when you act on it. Just because you feel fear doesn't mean you're a coward. You'll never find that in the Bible. God never tells us to keep from experiencing fear. He tells us to "fear not" often, because he knows we will be afraid. How can we not? We're human.

Instead, God does say: *Do not fear because I am with you.*[14] He encourages us, telling us we do not need to give in to fearful thoughts. Don't be pressured by fear because God is more powerful than anything that could even threaten to harm our souls. God never condemned me for feeling afraid on a turbulent flight all those years ago. But, for a while, choosing not to fly would be allowing that fear to control me. By choosing to face my fear and board a flight, I acted beyond my fear.

What are you afraid of today? I know people who are afraid of water, contracting an incurable disease, dogs, dying, failing, and on goes the list. I've known people who were afraid to leave their home, but they finally recognized living such a life was really no way to live. They decided to dominate fear instead of allowing fear to dominate their life. No matter what your fears are, it's time to identify them, confront them, and defeat them, because one thing is sure: God's best for you is not to live in fear. In fact, he promises to help you get free. "I prayed to the Lord, and he answered me. He freed me from all my fears."[15]

My mother is a champion over fear. She was diagnosed with cancer at forty-eight years old and given only a few weeks to live. Daily, she told us later, she had to fight fearful thoughts of dying. The thing that helped her most, she said, was she kept moving. In faith that God had a plan for her even during such a trying time, she continued to cook, clean, and attend all of Lakewood's church services. She refused to allow fear to paralyze her and to put her in bed for the rest of her days.

She could have given in to thoughts like *I won't live until Christmas. I won't live to see my children grow up and get married. Just give up and go on and plan your funeral.* But she knew such foreboding trains of thought would leave her second-guessing everything. Instead she wanted what God promises: to grant us peace, sound thoughts, goodness. Thirty years later, my mother is still healthy and strong. She knows how living in truth makes the most of our time and enables God to get us to the *more* he has in mind for us. Our days are numbered, the Bible reminds us, and the wise person is the one who decides to make the most of every day, not to waste even one on a lie.[16]

Faith over Fear Frees You

Remember my fear of flying? If I had never boarded another plane, I would have missed so much in life.

In the last year alone, overcoming that fear of flying enabled me to travel more easily across the nation, even to Australia, in order to share the good news of all God does for us, how he loves us. And flying enabled a woman name Karen to approach me at a conference where I spoke in New Orleans—the very place my mission to Australia began.

You see, Karen had flown all the way from Australia to New Orleans to hear me speak. I was so touched and encouraged by her endeavor that when she asked me to speak at her conference, I didn't have to think twice. Of course! I was excited to go to a place that I had never been and, by God's grace, to make a difference in the lives of many people. Afraid of flying? No way! Going to Australia is part of my purpose in life.

God has helped me so much in this area that our family even took a vacation, traveling on September 11. Some people couldn't believe we would fly on the first anniversary of the day that planes were overtaken to be used essentially as bombs against our country. But our family knew the Lord was with us—and he was. Neither the airports nor the planes were very crowded! The airline staff was especially kind and caring. We not only made it safely, but the flight was enjoyable.

I was reminded once again you cannot let fear stop you. I could have been paralyzed by my personal fear of flying, or by our national fear of what happened that fateful day in 2001. But I would have missed so much: the quick trip to a great vacation with my family—and the ease of getting there and home again, too.

Sometimes, though, fear stops us in our tracks. We bail on something or someone because we're scared of the consequences, and when we bail we leave ourselves and others hurting.

One of the first times my husband and I went snowmobiling, we were brought by a guide to the top of a very steep hill. The mountain paths were beautiful, winding through aspen trees that captivated my attention. At the top, though, the only thing that arrested my sight was the long drop down. I couldn't even see the slope. As I approached the top, I watched as the other snowmobilers ahead seemed to disappear into thin air.

Fear settled in the pit of my stomach. I got scared and I thought: *I am not doing this. I am going to stop and let Kevin drive me down.* So when I tried to stop my snowmobile so suddenly, it began to slide sideways on the slippery snow and ice. Then fear took over. I knew that I was going down that slope, like it or not. I thought, *This snowmobile may be going down, but it's not taking me with it!* I quickly bailed off the machine. I jumped—and pronto. My plunge into the snow was cartoonworthy.

Meanwhile, my snowmobile took off down the hill. All. By. Itself.

That is exactly how fear works when we let it. We end up, stopped in our tracks out in the cold, while fear and the chaos that comes with it run amuck, threatening to cost us dearly and others (even the poor trees).

Fortunately for me that day, as I imagined how much money it would take to replace that snowmobile after it crashed into the trees, the machine stopped on its own. No one was hurt, except my own ego. It turned out I was the joke of the trip that day, and Kevin has never let me live that one down.

God wants to free us from all that. Fear will hold us back from enjoying the exhilarating thing God has for each of us. Fear tells us: *You're not qualified to do what God has called you to do. You won't make it. You'll fall. The drop will be deep and it will hurt too much. Let someone else go ahead or do the driving.*

But God says: *Hang on, because I'm with you. Isn't this beautiful, this path I've brought you on, just for you? Look how far you can go! See how free you can fly when you keep going with me by your side!*

God Offers His Help and Hand

That is God's promise, remember? To help us, hold us up, and keep his victorious hand on us.

To grasp his victorious hand means we have a bit of a fight on our own hands first. It's not so easy to simply stop fear, right? I chose to trust God in the midst of all my fear following the mail bomb explosion, but a choice wasn't all it took. My anxious thoughts didn't disappear just because I decided I wanted that.

Yet—and this is important—deciding to reject fear is a first step to victory, an essential step. You have to claim that choice and resolve in your heart to believe in God's promise: *You are made for more than living a life crippled by fear and unable to fulfill your destiny.* Then you need to make that choice again. And again. It is a process, steps on the journey of faith.

This isn't always easy. Once I was racing through the airport with Kevin to make a flight after already spending a long day traveling. We feared we would miss our flight—and also our dinner, as we hadn't eaten in hours. So we rushed across the airport from one flight to the next, stopping quickly along the way to buy a hot dog each. Then we kept running through the airport, hot dogs in hand.

Or so I thought.

We finally made it on board. As we got ready to settle into our seats, I realized my dinner was missing.

Oh no! I was already starving. I couldn't go another few hours without something to eat. I panicked and stood up, blurting, "Where's my hot dog?!"

Everyone on board turned to look at me as Kevin tugged at my elbow. "Lisa," he said, quietly embarrassed. "You gave it to me to hold, remember?"

I sat down, equally embarrassed. I had! Everything was fine.

That is the way it is so often with things we fear in life: God's got ahold of them for us. He's looking out for us. But we have trouble truly handing over our care to him, or we think somehow, maybe even subconsciously, that we need to grab them back. All along, things are just fine—in fact, better—in his hands. We just need to choose again and again to place every care, every fear, in his control.

Once I made that decision, I would replace every negative thought that came with something Paul of the Bible said: "I can do all things through Christ who strengthens me."[17] I refused to live in fear. Then I would combat fears that threatened to keep me from even routine things by continuing to do what I had always done before the explosion. If an anxious thought whispered in my ear *Don't go out because there might be a bomb waiting,* I would go out anyway. If a fear told me not to drive that day because a bomb might be under the car, I drove anyway. Every fear was replaced with a step of faith.

I stared down every anxious thought and said, "God, I choose to trust you to take care of me." I determined to take each step and go to work and live as always, with one exception:

The church bought a new mail scanner!

Five Steps of Faith to Overcome Fear

Staring down every anxious thought takes some intention. That means you have to be deliberate and remind yourself of these five practices:

1. Recognize you control your response

In the trials of life, you decide what your response will be—no one else can do that for you. When fear presents itself and that panic button pops up in your mind, remind yourself: "I have a choice here. I can choose to panic, or I can choose faith and peace and joy instead."

To panic means you allow yourself to be overcome by sudden fear. But God made you not to be overcome but an overcomer. That means you don't bail like I did on that snowmobile. You don't pull out the white flag of surrender to your fears. Instead, you stay the course. You meet fear face-to-face with faith, since you can't conquer what you can't confront.

You can't confront what you are unwilling to identify. Identify the fears in your life, and let these thoughts know they are not going to live in your mind rent free any longer. Maybe you're thinking, *Some thoughts have lived in my mind for so long, they could be drawing Social Security by now.* You can still choose today as the time to stop fearful and panicky thoughts. You say to God, "I'm going to trust you to bring me through" and when anxiousness begins to rise, you say it again. And again.

Take heart in Jesus's encouragement: *Do not let your heart be troubled. Rely on me.*[18] Visualize Jesus taking that panic button from you. He's offering to hold it anyway. You might be thinking: *It's not enough to simply have faith that God is in control—I need him here, right now, right here beside me.* Well, he is. He promised to never forsake you.[19] Do you believe? It is a choice.

2. Listen to your spirit, not your head

When fears come, so do an array of emotional, negative thoughts. This is not the time to make decisions based on how you feel, because your emotions will take you up, down, and all over the place.

It's not the time to try and reason out everything, either. This is our natural bent—to want to know why and how, when and where. Too often we waste so much energy trying to figure out things only God knows. We have to be careful that we don't obsess over things we can't figure out or understand, or take ownership of worry, which causes us to panic. Jesus said: *Why worry about what to eat or drink or wear?*[20] That's taking ownership of and trying to reason out all the wrong things. That's when fear or worry causes us to dwell on thoughts like *What am I going to do? What is God going to do?*

What if we didn't need to know everything? Wouldn't we be free to live for this moment, for a purpose?

One time I was talking to my friend Debra about something that was bothering me. After elaborating and going into great detail, I said to her, "So what do you think?" I will never forget what her response was: "Lisa, I think you think too much!" She was right! Many times we read too much into things and assume the worst, and if we are not careful we will begin to be anxious or fearful about things that will never happen. Don't overthink things. You cannot solve every worry.

You can simplify your life by simplifying your thoughts.

Next, think on this: God tells us, *Be still and know that I am God.*[21] Lean on, trust in, and be confident in the Lord with all your heart and do not rely on your own understanding.[22] That means be still in your mind, which is so limited in insight and understanding. God is sovereign and he knows all things. Simplify your thinking by letting go of a need to know all the whys and hows, the whens and wheres. Focus on knowing that God knows everything about your present and your future, and he loves you and wants the best for you.[23] Trusting in this will bring you a supernatural peace that will be available to you in the midst of the storm.

3. Replace worry with prayer

You can fret over your situation, but worry will do nothing. Or you can pray to Almighty God—the one who has the power to do something about your situation and longs to help you. Prayer is so simple, yet many times we make it hard. Prayer is talking to God like he is our best friend, because he is—and he's not looking for fancy, eloquent language, nor is he timing the length of our prayers. He looks at the sincerity in our heart and he listens to our every word. Many times we turn to prayer as a last resort when things are not going right, but God tells us: *Turn to prayer first and you will find peace.*[24]

4. Remove the words fear and afraid from your vocabulary

Listen to what you are saying. You can go around saying, "I'm afraid, I'm afraid, I'm afraid!" But what if you replaced every *afraid* with *believe* and *know*?

What if you said, "God, I believe you will see me through."

Or, "I believe you are with me in this and are more powerful than any trouble."

Or, "I know you will show me a way through and get me to something better."

Speak the truth that God is more powerful than any fear you may have.

TO HELP YOU MORE

Safe in the Father's Hands

One of the sweetest memories I have about my earthly daddy is that he loved to hold hands. Even as an adult, as Daddy and I walked together, he would reach over and hold my hand just like he did when I was a child. I loved it!

I remember one time, when we were younger, our parents took us on a mission trip to Guadalajara. Our whole family slept in cots in a room together, and one night I slept next to Daddy. I'll never forget that as we lay down, he took hold of my hand and held it until I fell asleep. That was a comfort to me because we were in a strange place. When we woke up in the morning, he was still holding my hand. I felt safe in my daddy's hands.

A few days before Daddy passed away, he and my mother came over for dinner. After we ate, we sat in the family room to visit. I was sitting sideways in our recliner and I had my hand propped up on the back of the chair. Daddy came over and placed his hand on mine. He held it and caressed it while I visited with my mother. I'll never forget his loving touch. That was the last time he ever held my hand.

My earthly daddy is in Heaven and I miss him, but I know that I am not alone. There is someone else who is holding my hand every day of my life, and that is my Heavenly Father. I hope you know he holds your hand, too.

There are many wonderful Scriptures that talk about our Heavenly Father's hands.

1. **Your Heavenly Father is holding your hand.** Psalm 73:23 says, "Yet I am always with you; you hold me by my right hand." You may not know what it's like to walk hand in hand with your earthly father, because some of you never had that privilege. Take comfort in the fact that your Heavenly

Father is holding your hand and he never lets go.

2. **The Father guides us with his hand.** As God holds your hand, he directs your steps. We can trust him to guide us through life—through decisions, through conflicts, and through trials and tribulations. But we have to let him take the lead and trust him to know what is best for our lives. Psalm 31:14–15 says, "But I trust in you, O Lord; I say, you are my God. My times are in your hands."

3. **The Father molds and shapes us with his hand.** His hand is a transforming hand. Isaiah 64:8 says, "Yet, O Lord, you are our Father. We are the clay, you are the potter; we are the work of your hand." He is always working to improve us, molding and making us. Like a potter, God will put pressure on us in the areas of our lives that we need to change. We must learn to be pliable and flexible in the hands of the master potter, allowing him to smooth out our rough edges.

4. **The Father's hand sustains us.** Psalm 18:35 says, "Your right hand sustains me." *Sustain*

means "to hold up, to support, to encourage," and "to keep from falling or sinking." God will hold you up with his mighty hand and support you and keep you from falling. When you lie down at night thinking you can't make it another day, remember what Psalm 3:5 says: "I lie down and sleep; I wake again, because the Lord sustains me." You can make it and you will make it because of your Heavenly Father's sustaining hand.

5. **The Father's hand is a saving hand.** Psalm 138:7 says, "Though I walk in the midst of trouble, you preserve my life; you stretch out your hand against the anger of my foes, with your right hand you save me." You may be in a trial now that seems overwhelming, but you can know that God's hand is not too short to help you and rescue you.

6. **The Father's hand is an open hand.** God's hand is not closed to you, as many people assume. Psalm 145:16 says, "You open your hand and satisfy the desires of every living thing." When our children were just babies, they couldn't walk or talk or eat by themselves. But one thing they learned to do was

to simply lift up their little hands for help. What were they doing? Saying, *Mommy, hold me. Daddy, I need you.* As God's dear children, we must learn to lift up our hands to our Heavenly Father. His hand is open to you—take hold of it. Let him be the father you never had. Let him hold you, carry you, and take care of you.

5. Act in faith despite fear

Knowing that fear is the opposite of faith will empower you to act against fear. Whatever fear tells you, do the opposite! If fear tells you that you can't do it, then do it anyway. When you step out in faith, God will step out with you. I have learned that courage is a decision, not a feeling. If we wait for the feeling of courage, we may never act against fear. Most courageous acts are actually done in fear and trembling. As I chose to get back on the airplane over and over again, it didn't feel good, but I remembered the words of God to Joshua. "Do not fear, but be strong and courageous."[25]

You see, Moses had died and God chose Joshua to take his place of leadership. It was a tall order to follow in the footsteps of such a great leader, and God knew the pressure that Joshua felt. He told Joshua the same thing three times, but the last time he said, *Have I not commanded you? Be strong and courageous. Do not be afraid; do not be discouraged, for the* LORD *your God will be with you wherever you go.*[26]

This is what God is saying to you today: *My command to you is to be strong and very courageous to confront your fear. Don't obey fear—obey me because I will be with you, too.* The Bible says that God has given us not a spirit of fear, but a spirit of power, love, and self-discipline.[27] He has commanded us to act against fear and equipped us to be courageous.

God promises: *I will be with you; and when you pass through the rivers, they will not sweep over you. When you walk through the fire, you will not be burned; the flames will not set you ablaze.*[28]

God's Got a Hold on You

As I used these practices to stare down my fears, I kept reminding myself of a beautiful promise God makes us: *I'm on your side. Don't be afraid. What can man do to you that I cannot redeem?*[29]

That promise alone helped me when fear would creep into my everyday life. It reminded me of what

Jesus told his disciples: "Men's hearts will fail them because of fear."[30]

That's the worst thing fear sets out to do: give you heart failure or cause your spirit to faint and take the courage out of you. But just because we feel faint or that our heart is failing doesn't mean God is not in control. He is with us in our darkest hour, offering to hold us, help us, and keep his hand on us. Jesus was with me when my lights went out in the explosion, and he was with people who reached out to him in faith over fear long ago.

In one of my favorite stories in the Bible, Jesus is crossing by boat from one side of a lake to the other.[31] A large crowd gathered round him, and a church ruler fell at Jesus's feet needing a miracle. The ruler's daughter was dying.

He begged Jesus: "Come put your hands on her and she will live." The ruler knew there was power in even a touch of Jesus's hand.

So did a woman following along. She needed healing, having suffered with an affliction for years, but she could have been afraid to even ask for it. The unwell were not received gladly by crowds like the one surrounding Jesus that day. Besides, she might have told herself anxiously, there were so many others asking for miracles ahead of her. Who was she anyway to ask for one? But she believed in God's promise to keep his victorious hand out to us, to hold us and help us. So she reached out, fighting through any fears, and touched the hem of Christ's robe.

And she was healed.

Jesus looked at her right away. There were so many people reaching out to him, touching his sleeve, bumping against his shoulder, asking for miracles as he headed to the church ruler's house to make one happen. But he knew exactly who had touched his robe, who had reached out to him. He knows every need requested. He knew this woman's need like he knows yours. He knows when you're scared or anxious in the crowd. He is ready to offer his hand, and even his hem.

So he healed the woman along his way to the ruler's house.

By the time he got to the ruler's house, though, the daughter had died. Everyone was wailing and moaning. There was quite the commotion.

Jesus is ready to offer his hand and even his hem.

We're afraid you're too late, he was told.

Hold on, he told the people. "Don't be afraid, just believe."

Jesus is never too late. He knows just when we need his help most. He took the ruler's daughter by the hand and told her to get up. And she not only got up, she walked around.

I love this story because it shows how Jesus had more in mind for this girl and her family—and the woman he met along the way, and all the people hearing and seeing these miracles. He had more in mind for them just like he has more in mind for us, if we will just choose faith over fear.

Simple faith led that church ruler to Jesus, and simple faith gave both an older woman and a young girl new lives.

Simple faith can do something new for you today, too. Faith will go with you through the dark places. Faith will help you press through the fears that crowd your mind. Faith will help you hold on to the hand of God, and when you don't feel his hand you can know Jesus is with you and he offers his hem, because you are made for more than a slow death by fear. You are made to go boldly into this world. You are made to fear not, for God is with you.

7

Finding More
When You're Disappointed

*Because You're Made for Fulfillment, Not
Failure*

∞

Before Kevin and I got married, we had lots of long
talks about the major relationship issues. You know:
finances, jobs, in-laws, even out-laws! (Yes, we agreed,
we were each opposed to a life of crime.) We decided
mutually on things, like I would never expect him to
preach or work in ministry and he would support the
fact I was a preacher in ministry. We talked openly
about our desires and made sure we were compatible
and on the same page.

Imagine my surprise, then, when one year after
our marriage Kevin told me that he felt a desire to
work at the church. He had been in management at
a top construction firm and was very content with
his job. He had even politely turned down my father the previous year, when Daddy expressed a wish
for Kevin to work at the church because we needed
someone with his capacity. I was fine with that. I

wanted Kevin to be happy in his work.

When Kevin wanted to work with the church, I admit I was beyond fine again. I was thrilled. This was doubly good icing on an already delicious cake, to work in tandem directly with my husband to make a difference in this world together.

But things don't always go like we expect. No matter how much you talk something through, or plan, or carefully go a certain way, disappointments will come.

The Anticipation That Leads…Nowhere

One of the big things we'd talked through before marriage was our feeling about children. Kevin and I were definitely on the same page. We each loved children and wanted at least three, probably more, of our very own. Being a twin, Kevin always had a desire to have twins, though we knew the likelihood of that wasn't so good. (Genetically, a male fraternal twin isn't as likely to have twins himself.)

So we were excited to start our family.

After three years of marriage, though, we weren't having any success. We sought medical advice. I had exploratory surgery, which showed I had extensive endometriosis and scar tissue on my uterus. Probably, doctors said, the scar tissue was a result of the mail bomb explosion.

In any case, as long as I had all that scar tissue, I couldn't carry a baby.

Over the next three years, I had two corrective surgeries and began the fertility process. After that, I was in and out of a great fertility clinic. I went through it all: the hormones, the shots, in-vitro fertilization. I felt like the clinic was my second home. Trying to start our family was a busy and continual process.

After a failed attempt at in-vitro fertilization, the doctor called Kevin and me into his office. We would discuss the next step. Or so I thought. Little did we know that we were about to be hit with a ton of bricks.

I will never forget those next five minutes. That was how fast our visit happened. I can replay those five minutes in my mind in slow motion, and they still seem so clipped, so short. Our doctor looked at Kevin, then me, and said frankly: "Lisa, we have tried to help you, but enough is enough. There comes a time when you have to get the h—— on with your life! We don't think we can do anything else to help you."

I felt smacked by the first brick. Both Kevin's and my faces dropped in shock.

The doctor continued: "And Lisa, here is the name of a psychiatrist. I think you are going to have to make an appointment with her."

Wow.

Ouch.

The whole wall of proverbial bricks fell, every brick socking me hard on the head and in the stomach. Kevin and I walked out of the clinic in disbelief, not only because of what the doctor said but how he said it. Outside, it wasn't just the crisp October air that stung our faces. It was the doctor's blunt, quick delivery of this unexpected news.

Then the first thing Kevin said to me was, "Lisa, don't be discouraged, because our trust has never been in man, but in God."

Thank God for an encouraging husband. I agreed with him. I knew he was right. We believed in God's power and goodness. We had seen him at work in our lives numerous times.

Still, in the coming six months I spiraled into a deep darkness.

By winter, I began to experience physical symptoms of my emotional state. Only I didn't see it that way. Often, I would wake in the night with my heart racing. Twice I had a short burst of what I thought was claustrophobia. I dismissed each incident with a series of excuses. I was working too hard. Things were busy. This was just some passing illness....

Then the symptoms escalated. I began to have full-blown panic attacks that scared me. This was not like my optimistic self at all. Was something wrong with my mind? Was I going crazy? Maybe I needed to take a break from work. I changed from being an energetic, outgoing person to not wanting to go anywhere or do anything.

Looking back, Kevin and I realized I had been putting an enormous demand on my body with all the fertility treatments, and my body was saying: *I've had enough!* My spirit was strong, but my body was weak. My mind was burdened, too. I had heaped a heavy load of guilt onto my stress level. I took all the blame for our inability to start a family. *After all,* I told myself, *Kevin was not the problem. I was. I could not give him children. I may never be able to give him children.*

Even though I knew—I believed!—that with God, all things are possible, I felt trapped in a field of disappointment. I couldn't do anything about this. What a hopeless feeling. How lonely were those fields that once seemed ripe with promise and turned suddenly to vacant lots.

Alone in the Fields of Disappointment

You know those places. How many times in life are we led to these fields? Things don't turn out the way we plan. You don't get that promotion. The loan for buying that house doesn't go through. The vacation you counted on gets wiped away by too many pressing bills, too much to do, and no left over time or money. The friend you counted on doesn't call. The one you thought you'd grow old with leaves you for someone younger. No matter how much you work out, that tummy bulge never seems to leave.

Each of us faces such disappointments at one time or another. It's so easy to become overwhelmed by them. You begin to wonder if you'll ever have the bright future you so deeply desire. You long for some hope, some peace.

In such times of disappointment, confusion, and darkness, I've discovered God's truth can take over and light a way. That's because God doesn't waste a single thing in our lives, not the weeds, not the thorns, nor the brambles. Not even the dirt.

TO HELP YOU MORE

Let God Dream a Bigger Dream for You

When I was still going through the fertility process, I was so focused and determined to have children. Kevin and I prayed earnestly and continued to put our hope and trust in God. But after six years, I came to a place of surrender because the will and want to have children was consuming my life, all my thinking.

For me, surrender meant I got on my knees

and prayed: "Father, I have asked about children for all these years, but I want you to know that if I never have children, I will still love you and serve you with all my heart. I want you to know that I am grateful for all that I do have: a wonderful husband, home, job, family, and friends. What I want more than anything is to do your will. I will never pray about children again because I release that burden today."

Many times we think of surrender as giving up on our hopes and dreams. That's not at all what my prayer was or what surrender means. What surrender means is allowing God, who knows us better than we know ourselves, to dream a bigger dream than ours. We still hope and we still dream and we still bring those things to God, but we become willing to leave them in his tender hands knowing he will give us back something even better.

This isn't an easy prayer, but it is a true one that lets God know, more than anything else, he is first in our lives. And our lives are precious to him—he promises to show us what more he has in store.

You may be thinking: *I have prayed and done everything I know to do, but nothing has changed. What's wrong? Am I doing all of this for nothing?*

No, you're not! The truth is, God takes every heartache, every difficulty, each bad result, and tends it, turns it around just like a farmer tills a field and transforms it all for good, for a plentiful harvest. The key is to keep your trust in God, who is not limited by your circumstances or inabilities.

Jesus said: "I have told you these things, so that in me you may have [perfect] peace and confidence. In the world you have tribulation and trials and distress and frustration; but be of good cheer [take courage; be confident, certain, undaunted]! For I have overcome the world. [I have deprived it of power to harm you and have conquered it for you]."[1]

That means the jobless one finds work after a year of unemployment.

The insurance covers the expense to repair your wrecked car.

The physical therapy helps you stand on that broken ankle once more.

The barren find fullness.

Only a few of these things come about in the way we expect.

Five Truths to Get You to Goodness

That's why getting to the places of not only hope,

but hope realized requires a journey. On a journey, you take one step at a time. These steps will get you through fields of disappointment to the mountaintops God means for you to reach. Each step will give you a greater understanding of your destiny too.

1. Don't blame God—run to him

Isn't it so tempting when things go wrong to look for someone to blame? God never promised that our lives would be trouble free. Sometimes, bad things happen to good people. When unexpected trouble or tragedy comes, God is not the cause. He is not against us. He is for us.

Remember what Jesus said: "In this world, you will have trouble."[2] But he encourages you, "Don't despair, don't give up because I have overcome the world."

In despair it helps to focus on just one thing at a time. You may not have energy for much more. So focus on the fact that God is good all the time. What you are going through may be bad. The circumstances may be terrible. You may not feel good, but God is good. He is not the source of confusion, trouble, or evil.[3] He is so much more. Look at these descriptions of him by people who have experienced him before us: He is:

- our anchor.[4]
- our hope.[5]
- our peace.[6]
- our wisdom.[7]
- our deliverer and way of escape.[8]

There is only one who can truly deliver you from and heal disappointment. The Bible says our help comes from the Lord, the maker of Heaven and earth.[9]

God offers us safety and shelter from the storms of life. Run to him, not from him! God's plan is always to prosper you, not to harm you.[10] He says: *Draw near to me and I will draw near to you.*[11]

Recognize today that God is at work in your life and he has kept you from more trouble and harm than you will ever know. Trust that he is good and that he will carry you through any difficulty you may face.

2. Trust God's wisdom, even when things don't make sense to your mind

When you're disappointed it's so easy to get stuck on asking why:

Why did this happen to me?

What did I do wrong?

Why do I have to suffer? I'm a good person. I serve God!

Why me, Lord?

And on and on. The truth is, some things we will never know or understand this side of Heaven. Trusting God doesn't mean you'll always have all the answers. In fact, if you did have all the answers, you wouldn't need to trust God. That's why the Bible says, *Don't rely on your own insight and understanding.* Whether we understand a situation or not does not change God nor his character. "The secret things belong to the LORD our God, but the things revealed belong to us."[12] If God doesn't reveal something to you then he must have a reason, because the secret things belong to him.

I like David's attitude in Psalm 131:1–2: "I do not concern myself with great matters, Nor with things too profound for me. Surely I have calmed and quieted my soul." David understood that he may not get all the answers to his questions. He also understood that if he kept asking *why,* he would be drawn into a vortex of confusion and anxiety. Instead, David calmed his own soul by putting his trust in God.

When you face adversity, you can do the same. You can choose to lay aside the unanswered questions and let your soul be calmed and quieted. You can be still and know that God is God. You can trust his faithfulness and goodness, and that he always has your best interest at heart. You can choose to move forward and not let your questions keep you from your destiny.

I've found that there are times when we look back on our lives and thank God that things didn't turn out the way we wished. That job you so desperately wanted may have consumed you and not really helped pay the bills. That car you thought would answer your transportation prayers may have been a costly clunker. The date you set your hopes on may have brought you, instead of roses, a dozen griefs.

Sometimes we realize that what we asked for or wanted isn't really what we needed, nor is it God's best plan for our life. We go through things that we don't understand today, but we will understand better in the future. We will be able to look back and see God's wisdom—how he wasn't punishing or overlooking us, but sparing and saving us. We will see that he was directing our steps all along. Trust that even when you don't always know what's best for your life (and even when you think you do), God always does.

3. Expect God to comfort you

You don't have to be in a relationship with a person very long to be disappointed by that person. Sometimes it's something minor, like they are late to meet you, or they forget your birthday. Other times the reasons are more painful: that person lies to you or outright betrays you. People may hurt you, disappoint you, defy you, or reject you, but God never will. He is full of love and compassion. He promises to comfort you in all your troubles.[13]

When children are little, they fall down and scratch their knee just a little bit, but cry and scream as if their legs are broken. But when you sit them on your lap and bring out a Band-Aid with Winnie the Pooh on it, then suddenly everything is all right. They don't hurt anymore. They don't cry anymore. They are as happy as can be, and they run off to show that Band-Aid to everyone they see.

God is the same way with us. When we face a disappointment in life, we can crawl into the lap of Father God. He will hold and comfort us. He will let us cry awhile and listen to our fears and calm our hearts like no one else can. All it takes is one touch from our Heavenly Father, just like that Band-Aid, to know that everything is going to be all right. His love is so much greater than our pain.

TO HELP YOU MORE

Share Your Hope and God Will Harvest Hope for You

The Bible tells us that we reap whatever we sow. In other words, what you make happen for others, God will make happen for you. When you encourage others, you will be encouraged.

When you lift someone's spirit, God will lift your spirit. When you love someone in the midst of their difficulty, God will make sure you are loved through yours.

Something powerful happens when you begin to help others out of your own needs and disappointments. The Bible specifically mentions ten things God will do (Isaiah 58:8–11, NLT):

1. Your light will break forth like the morning.
2. Your healing will come quickly.
3. Your godliness will lead you forward (not backward!).
4. The glory of the Lord will protect you from behind.
5. When you call, the Lord will quickly answer.
6. Your light will shine out from the darkness, and the darkness around you will be as bright as day.
7. The Lord will guide you continually.
8. He will water your life when you are dry.
9. He will keep you healthy.
10. You will be like a well-watered garden, like an ever-flowing spring that never goes dry.

These aren't just pretty ideas. They are the promises of God—and they are for every person who dares to look past his or her own needs and reach out to others with the same love God gives us.

4. Don't compare your life to others

It's easy to keep your focus on how good other people have it. You'll run into people who don't seem to have problems like you do. They seem happy and blessed all the time. But not you—you start looking at their load and compare it to your heavy load. Before long, you've put the cherry of self-pity on top of your sundae of despair.

This is what David began to do in Psalm 73. He basically said: "Lord, I'm in so much trouble, but when I look at other people I become envious. They are prosperous. They have no struggles. Their bodies are healthy and strong. It seems like I have kept a pure heart in vain."

Have you ever thought that? *God, I've done everything right and I still have trouble!*

But David realized he was going down the wrong path. He had to change his thought process. He said, "When I try to understand all of this it is oppressive for me!"[14]

When we compare ourselves to others, we become oppressed and depressed. Comparison isn't healthy physically, spiritually, or emotionally. We can get derailed from getting to where God wants us, living abundantly. Imagine trying to drive somewhere that you've never been and instead of following your own GPS system, you try to follow the GPS system inside the car next to you. Sound crazy? It is! You don't even know where that car is headed. How can you possibly expect their directions to help you reach your destination? You have to mind your own steering wheel, your own business; run your own race, follow your own destiny. Every person has his or her own battles to conquer.

God will keep you in perfect peace as you trust in him.[15] In your disappointments, if you keep your thoughts fixed on God and not other people, he will keep you in that place of perfect peace.

5. In your time of need, meet someone else's need

Even when you don't feel your best, or strongest, you still have something to give. Focusing on helping others gets your eyes off yourself and your problems. It helps you realize that you aren't the only one who is hurting, which can keep you from isolating yourself and wallowing in self-pity. I made an effort to pray for and encourage others who were facing infertility. I sowed seed in my need by babysitting others' children. This helped me get my eyes off myself, gave me great experience with children, and blessed others, too.

6. Don't worry about changing what you cannot change

As much as we hate to accept it at times, there are just some things in life that we cannot change. For starters, we definitely can't change people. (I've been trying to change my husband for twenty-one years and I haven't been successful yet!) Sometimes we can't change circumstances, the doctor's report, or the fact that a child has gone astray. The good news is that we serve a God who can.

"With man this is impossible, but with God all things are possible."[16]

That doesn't mean we just sit back in a lounge chair and do nothing. No, we need to do all we can do, and trust God to do what we cannot do. Remember God will never leave you stranded when you put your trust in him.

How God Takes the "Dis" and Leaves You an "Appointment"

See that is the amazing thing about disappointing places. God will not leave you in them. He will redeem them by using them to give you things you could not have otherwise: a job only you can do, a story only you can tell, a fight only you can win. He will turn your field of sorrow into one of splendor, your battlefield into a place of blessing, your mess into a message.

A friend once told me, "Lisa, in your disappointment, you can discover God's appointment."

This kind man was saying: God will remove the "dis" and give you his "appointment."

That was exactly what happened for Kevin and me. We couldn't change our situation, but we could focus on the fact that God was not limited by our circumstances.

So even though we were sad, even though we too wondered why, we decided to let God do what he would do, and we would do what only we could do. We read God's Word and reread his promises, "Children are a reward from God."[17] Kevin and I knew that God would not withhold this reward from us. We set our hearts to trust God to fulfill this promise in spite of our negative circumstances, and to keep our faith in the God who performs miracles.

During this time, one day we got a sample of diapers in the mail. But the sample wasn't of just one diaper. There were two.

"Look, Lisa!" Kevin said, showing me the samples. "Two diapers for our twins!"

That was his faith talking. He put it in writing, too. He took a Sharpie pen and wrote on the package: "Our twins! December 17, 1993." Then he tucked away those little diapers like the promises from God we had tucked in our hearts. What faith Kevin had.

And what faithfulness God had to us, because all the while he was working behind the scenes on our behalf. He was setting events in order when I was in despair because I couldn't get pregnant.

He led me to wise counsel from a Christian doctor and friend, Dr. Reginald Cherry, who helped me walk through this season of my life with prayer and medicine for the anxiety.[18] And in the meantime, God was working on other details: the children we so much desired.

Kevin had always had a desire to have children and adopt children, but the desire to adopt was not something I entertained because I was intent on doing all I could to get pregnant. Kevin approached the subject again, saying, "Lisa, you know we can always adopt children."

I cut him off with a lament: "I know, but I don't want to go through another long process just to be rejected again."

Yet when I got alone, I prayed about this. I said, "God, only you know what is right. Kevin has a desire to adopt, but honestly I am tired and do not know what to do. I need your help because I love and respect my husband." I didn't want to close a door that God wanted to open. I prayed something next that I have never prayed before or since: "God, I need to have a supernatural sign from you, if adoption is your will." I was desperate and I needed clear direction.

God, in his tender mercy, sent one.

Every Baby Really Is a Miracle

A few years before my despair over infertility, I met Nancy Alcorn at a conference where we were both speakers. Nancy founded and leads Mercy Ministries, which offers help to troubled girls, and I was so touched by her story that I made a beeline after she finished speaking to meet her. She signed her book, *Echoes of Mercy*, for me and when I began to read it, I just couldn't put it down. The stories were amazing; they were about troubled girls finding freedom from addictions, low self-esteem, eating disorders, and other issues. Our family and church connected with Nancy, and we continue to support her wonderful ministry today.

But it never clicked with me that Nancy would be the angel bearing that supernatural message from God for me and for Kevin....

Not until she called. Her call was the first time we had connected in a long while, and she had no knowledge of what Kevin and I had been going through in trying to start our family.

Imagine my surprise, then, when Nancy said, "Lisa, I want you to know that this is not a call I would ordinarily make." She paused. "Do you and Kevin have children?"

"Not yet," I said.

"Well," she continued, "there is a seventeen-year-old girl who approached me because she is pregnant with twin girls and desires to find a godly home for them. She has some strict requirements for the potential parents. She's considered all the people who have applied to our ministry, and has not been able to make a decision."

My mind was already racing. *Twins?!*

"Lisa," Nancy said, "I have been concerned about this adoption because the girls will be born in June. I have prayed about this and I felt strongly to call and see if you and Kevin are interested." She paused again, then said, "Do you think you would be interested in adopting?"

I had listened silently, but by this time I was ready to come through that phone! "Interested?" I exclaimed. "Nancy, you save those babies for us and I am going to go tell Kevin the good news!" I was so happy I almost hung up on her, then ran down to Kevin's office. "You aren't going to believe what just happened!" I said, practically bursting with joy.

I explained the whole conversation and we just laughed and thanked God—because we could believe what just happened. We knew it was God who made it happen, because that's our God, the God of miracles, the God who exchanges hope for disappointment, the God who wants us to live expectantly.

"Go call Nancy back and tell her we are interested," Kevin said, beaming.

I beamed back. "I already did."

"Well, go call her again just to make sure!" he said.

For weeks after, we couldn't wipe the smiles off of our faces. Nor could we erase the wonder of how God brought our babies to us. First, not just a miracle baby but the twins Kevin prayed for; second, that we fit the birth mother's very specific requirements that the adopting couple:

1. are Christians,
2. work in the full-time ministry,
3. live in the South,
4. live around cousins and grandparents,
5. are under the age of forty, and
6. have twins in their family.

When Nancy mentioned the twin requirement she said, "I didn't know of any twins in your family, so I will talk to the birth mother about that. Maybe she'll release you from that requirement."

Release us!? I wanted to burst again. "Nancy," I said, my voice full of wonder, "I don't know if I ever told you, but Kevin is a twin."

This time Nancy almost came through the phone. No one could have orchestrated this miracle but God.

We began the adoption process, waiting in anticipation for the twins to be born.

TO HELP YOU MORE

God's Answers Are Always More

At the same time I was going through the fertility clinic, so was my friend, Ruth, who also longed for a child. Ruth went through the same type of treatments I did, and we often encouraged and prayed for each other. But Ruth had endometriosis even worse than I did. Getting pregnant seemed even less of a chance for her than it had for me.

Less than is in our human thinking. God always has more in mind than we can imagine. Not long after Kevin and I adopted the twins, Ruth told me she was pregnant; not only was she pregnant, but she and her husband, Tim, were having twin boys!

God answered both of our prayers, but in different ways.

That is why you can't compare what God is doing for others to what he is doing for you. God loves every person and is working for every person's best.

I could have wrestled with the comparison trap during the seven years before Kevin and I had children. My brothers and sisters all had children—and I am the oldest daughter. But my younger siblings were way ahead of me in this area. My friends were having babies all around me, too.

You might be in a situation like that, where it seems everyone around you is getting the answer you want. She has the husband you've longed for, or he got the promotion you've been working toward all these years.

I remember when my brother, Paul, said to me, "Lisa, I feel bad for you when I tell you we're having another baby. Does it make you feel sad because you haven't had children yourself?" It touched me. I said, "No, Paul, I am so happy because I get another nephew!" I was genuinely happy for them.

Colossians 2:7 encourages us to overflow with thankfulness, and I think it's interesting that the word *overflow* is used. Because when you overflow with gratitude, God's mercies start to flow into you. With gratitude, you begin to see the gifts around you: how they make that marriage work, how he got that promotion and is doing in that job. You learn that someone else's answer isn't yours to question but to celebrate. God is at work on just what you need, and he's going to deliver it in a way that wouldn't be right for anyone else but you—just as anyone else's answer was delivered to them in the way uniquely right for them.

For Kevin and I, all the celebrations we'd had of babies in our family's and friends' lives came back to us tenfold. I'd attended many a shower and we'd given many a baby gift, and now we were getting so much more in return. We didn't even have to buy Catherine and Caroline clothes for the first year. Everyone else supplied them with gifts.

The blessings of God will flow in different ways for each of us, but one thing remains the same: He is merciful and generous, and he knows what each of us needs beyond a doubt.

God Makes Every Appointment Amazing

Did you know between the time the fertility doctor

gave Kevin and me his talk and the arrival of our twins was exactly nine months?

How amazing is God to orchestrate this time for me as he would in a mother who was carrying her child to birth? Even with this detail, God was working behind the scenes. We just couldn't see it. I was at home pushing through those horrible anxiety attacks, but God was preparing our miracle.

In fact, even after we got the good news about the adoption, I still faced challenges with anxiety. There were times when I felt like I thought I would be an unfit mother, but deep down I believed I was made for more than that—and God was telling me I was made to be a great mother. I was finally able to hear him when, during this waiting period, I had to take a short sabbatical from work. I would hate to see Kevin get in the car and drive off because I didn't want to be left with the fear and sadness I felt. So I spent extra time reading and meditating on God's Word. I found all the Scriptures I could about barren women in the Bible who were blessed with children. I realized that Moses, Samuel, and Jesus were adopted. I began to increasingly put my faith and trust in God instead of how I felt. And when I went to church, I would smile by faith, not because I felt like it.

The amazing thing is faith turned into reality. God restored my joy and brought me out of a horrible pit. He gave me beauty for ashes, and gladness instead of the spirit of despair and heaviness.[19] He also gave me tremendous compassion for those who experience anxiety and panic attacks. I experienced this first-hand, and they are very real and scary. But I can tell you that they are temporary and you will overcome them, if you will put your trust in God.

One of the ways God did this was by using the wisdom of my earthly father in my life. During this time, my dad would take me for walks to get me out of the house and to encourage me. One time I said to him, "Daddy, I prayed and read my Bible all morning and I felt so good. But when I was finished, I felt bad again."

He said to me, "Lisa, victory doesn't always come overnight. You have to be consistent in doing the right thing, and you will break through with God's help."

The next day I got up and thought of my father's words, and I determined to stay positive. I decided to put my faith, not my feelings, at the forefront of the day. And I did that the next day and the next day. I kept saying, "Father, I thank you for giving me the victory in this situation. I know that you have more for me than anxiousness and I will not give up!" When I was tempted to feel discouraged and hopeless, I would remind myself of the promise in Psalm 113:9, "Father, I thank you for making me a happy mother of children!"

And faith and persistence worked. The anxiety eased a little every day, and as it eased, my faith grew.

You might say, "Lisa, how long did that take?"

Well, it took several weeks for me, but the point is it may take either longer or less time for you. But God is faithful. He will take your disappointment and give you a path to

> *Victory doesn't always come overnight. You have to be consistent in doing the right thing and you will break through with God's help.*

your destiny. He will take your "can't take it anymore" attitude and replace it with "I can make it." No matter what you are going through today, it is temporary and subject to change any day.[20]

You too can speak these words of faith every day over your own life and you will see them start to take hold:

I am going to make it!
I am made for more than living a life of defeat!
This season in my life is temporary!
I will fulfill my destiny!

Because God made you for more than disappointment and defeat.

When the adoption was final and we got the call from Nancy that our twins had arrived, Kevin and

I saw how much more God loved us. Though very little, the girls were healthy and strong. I became a happy mother of children, and Kevin was an ecstatic father! On the girls' fourth day, we brought them out of the hospital and to a hotel suite, where we'd set up house for ten days as the adoption papers were finalized. Our family members trickled in and out to see our beautiful babies, Catherine and Caroline.

Today our girls are thirteen years old.

When I think of how God made our family I am humbled and in awe. In fact, three years later God added Christopher to our family through another miracle delivered by Mercy Ministries, and our awesome son is ten years old today.

God is such a great God. He loves us so much, so tenderly. He cares about our dreams and the desires of our hearts, the desires he created in us. Nothing is beyond him.

If nothing is beyond him, you might think, *why didn't God just open your womb, Lisa, so you could have children?*

Honestly, I don't know why. But I do know God is capable of anything, everything. I know that, once again, God turned my *why?* into *wow!* I know he ordained, before the foundations of the world, that Catherine, Caroline, and Christopher would be ours—and having them is the greatest joy Kevin and I have ever known. I also like to joke that I sure don't mind that I didn't have to go through nine months of pregnancy and labor, and the delivery. We got our children and I got to keep my figure!

More than anything, I know this: God wants to do for you what he did for Kevin and me. It may be a mate you are desiring, not children—or a job, or a mission. You may not see how any of those things can come about because they haven't, no matter how hard you've tried to work for them to happen. But God can change what you cannot. He will turn your disappointments around and lead you into the bright future he has prepared for you. He will take the "dis" and give you an appointed story or message or mission.

Sometimes we go through things that we don't understand today, but we will understand better in the future. God may reveal it, or we will be able to look back and see God's wisdom and hand in our life. We will see that he was directing our steps all along. We don't always know what's best for our lives, but God does.

He gives you his Word: *As for me, my way is perfect.*[21] *Anyone who puts his trust in me will never be disappointed.*[22]

Of course, Kevin and I joke that we have a couple of sample diapers with that word, too. What an advertiser sent as a sample to us has become a memorial stone: twin diapers that proclaim, "Our twins!"

8

Finding More
When You Can't Let Go

Because You're Made to Move On—
and Move Mountains

∽

One summer my younger sister April, our mom, and I were holding down the fort while Daddy, Tamara, and Joel were on a mission trip, and Paul was away at medical school. Mother was at home when April and I, working at the church, got a call from a neighbor.

"Lisa," he said. "Your mother is all right, but your house caught fire and the firefighters are on the way!"

April and I jumped in the car and raced home, worried about mother and our house the whole way. We were supposed to be holding down the fort—and the fort was on fire!

From a distance we could see a crowd gathered on our street. As soon as we reached the edge of the crowd we put the car in park and hopped out to find our mother. Our neighbor was with her, and we all watched as the firefighters tirelessly fought the flames. The neighbor told how the hot water heater had exploded. He saw the fire and raced to the door. After knocking loudly, he discovered that our mother was in another part of the house, not even aware of the explosion or the fire.

We marveled at that, and that Mother wasn't hurt, as firefighters extinguished the last flames. When they finished, we looked over the damage. The outer structure was fine, but inside there were ashes, though more damage by smoke residue and water that had soaked everything from ceiling and walls to furniture and the floor. As we sifted through the rubble, we saw that some old pieces of furniture were beyond repair. Some could be reupholstered, but many were long worn out and overdue to get rid of anyway. What was most painful was finding precious treasures in our attic, like baby pictures, that were ruined. (I was surprised to find that my baby picture was damaged but salvageable, something I tease my brothers and sisters about as just another proof that I truly am the favorite!)

The bottom line was, the whole inside of our house needed to be gutted and rebuilt inside to be livable again. Until then, the only thing left standing would be the foundation and walls.

Getting Over and Going Through

The house fire was frightening. Though we felt spared from what could have been so much worse, we were sad at what went up in smoke. We had grown up in this house, and it was the only home we'd known in the Forest Cove subdivision of Humble, Texas.

But when we moved back into our house, it was as if we were living in a brand-new home! Walls were rebuilt and painted fresh. New carpet and flooring were in place. We even had some new furniture. It was amazing and a gift to our big family.

Isn't this just how our lives are? Many times we try to hang on to things, a habit or even a person, like an old piece of furniture. Hanging on ruins us. When something precious—a relationship, precious like an old baby picture—is ruined, we are devastated. We can stay stuck in the past, unable to let go. After frightening or terrible episodes in our lives, it's easy to hang on to the frustration, fear, anger or sadness. We can become bitter. We can play the "if only" game: *If only I'd worked harder. If only I'd been smarter. If only I were prettier. If only I gave more. If only I tried better. If only we'd checked that water heater…*

But the *ifs* don't change anything. They just keep us in the ashes. They make our future, like the past, go up in smoke. Dwelling on the *ifs* can make your days like a wasteland, covered in ashes, soaked with ruin—

or like a desert, endlessly dry and empty.

We fail to see how God, like a whole construction crew, will come upon the scene to build something brand-new onto our foundation, the very core of our lives. But if you turn to him and listen, you will hear it: the sound of hammers striking the nails against new wood, rebuilding everything in your life that has been lost, only this time creating something new, better, greater.

God says you are made for more than desert or wasteland living. Yes, he acknowledges, you will come to those places in life. But look at his promise: *Forget the former things. Do not dwell on the past. See, I am doing a new thing! Now it springs up; do you not perceive it? I am making a way in the desert and streams in the wasteland.*[1]

God has so much more in mind. He promises to make a way in your desert and bring streams, fresh and cleansing streams, to your wasteland. He wants to do something life-changing. He says it just like that, remember?

I want to do something new in your life.

Do you not perceive it?

Sadly, too much of the time we don't perceive it. We get stuck in the same rut, circumstances, or negative cycle. We stay fixed on our anger or frustration. We consume ourselves with the sadness. These are not easy things to give up, but what would happen if we did? What if we could get over the past and go through whatever was holding us back from perceiving the new thing God has for us?

If only—and this is a good *if*—we'd let go! In order to perceive what's new for our lives, we must forget some things, the former things that are too easy to dwell upon: loss, shame, guilt, hurt. How can we ever grab onto the future when we're holding on to the past?

TO HELP YOU MORE

A Picture of Letting Go and Letting God

A friend of mine, Gabriela, always knew she was destined to be a wife, mom, and photographer. She married Abel and they had three children. Soon Gabriela launched her photography business and was living her dream.

A few years down the road, though, her marriage began to feel stale. Abel worked twelve-hour-a-day shifts. Weekends were spent at the usual sporting events for their son. Even though Gabriela worked hard, she always stopped everything she was doing at 1:00 p.m. to prepare a great dinner for the family and keep the house spotless, mopping the tile floors, vacuuming, doing yard work. She thought she was being a good wife. This was what her mother did to keep her dad happy.

But Gabriela wasn't happy. She felt unappreciated and neglected as a wife, and tired and unfulfilled as a woman. *Abel and I are more like roommates,* she thought, *than husband and wife.* She began to think of divorce.

Then Gabriela received devastating news. Her doctor ordered bed rest for a heart condition. What happened to her destiny, she wondered, as photographer, mom, and wife? Was this it?

Instead of focusing on negative things and holding onto what used to be, however, Gabriela determined to hang on to the only things she knew to be true. First, she knew God wants more for us than misery. Second, she knew that she must let go of her negative thoughts about Abel and begin to take positive steps toward improving their marriage. She began to list Abel's positive attributes and do the things *she* could do to be a better wife and support to her husband.

With each step, barriers began to come down. When she talked more openly and lovingly to Abel, they began to really communicate in what seemed years. During one of their heart-to-heart talks, she discovered that Abel didn't care if she cooked every night or not. He was content with a take-out burger, and he had no idea how often she mopped or vacuumed.

Gabriela decided to take things a step further. She began sending Abel short, encouraging text messages while he was at work. She tucked away special love letters to give to him on occasions. She wrote him a letter asking his forgiveness for her shortcomings as a wife. She began to put more effort into their intimate relationship. "Before, I never even owned a piece of lingerie," she admits. All of that changed, too.

Step by step, over time, Gabriela's marriage came alive again. Though not overnight, her health returned.

When she looks back at how her destiny as a fulfilled and loving wife was almost derailed, she sees why. She thought her husband wanted cooked meals and a clean house, when what he wanted was so much more. What he really desired was time with his beautiful wife. And by letting go of the past and looking to the future, she opened her hands to the destiny God lovingly put in her hands.

Meet the Ambassador of Letting Go and Pressing On

That's a heavy list, isn't it? Shame and guilt, hurt and failure are so much a part of being human. But they are the bad part, the shackles that will weigh you down and tether you to only what's horrible or sad, the things that have gone up in smoke in your life.

The Apostle Paul speaks to us about this because he wrestled so much with these things. He was passionate all his life, and he had an intense past of hurt and violence. In fact, he could be called an ambassador of such shackles. Letting go was a lesson Paul had to learn.

He told the Philippians: "Not that I have already obtained all this, or have already been made perfect, but I press on to take hold of that for which Christ Jesus took hold of me. Brothers, I do not consider myself yet to have taken hold of it. But one thing I do: Forgetting what is behind and straining toward what is ahead, I press on toward the goal to win the prize for which God has called me heavenward in Christ Jesus."[2]

Isn't that beautiful? *I press on.*

"Right," you may say, "but did the Apostle Paul get burned by an ex? Was he wronged by a coworker? Did he feel wounded by someone he deeply loved?"

Well, actually, yes. Paul was wronged and he also

wronged others to an extreme. He was hurt and he also wounded others, even Christ, whom he came to love and devote his remaining days to.

Yes, Paul had a lot to forget. And God knew that. But God loved Paul and had a plan for his life. Even as Paul was working against God and declared Jesus an enemy, God revealed himself to Paul as he was traveling on the road to Damascus. With love and mercy, God did a new thing that would change this man's passion from bad to good and for good, as in forever.

In the very instant that God showed himself, Paul was blinded. The goodness of God is so bright. It was in that light, in his own blindness by it, that the apostle began to really see. Paul saw that he was made for more, that God had bigger things in mind for his life. He saw that his past of persecuting God's people did not disqualify him from doing a good thing and fulfilling his purpose and destiny.

That was when Paul really began to live with a passion. He got it. He let go of his past failures and mistakes, his frustrations and fears, and pressed forward.

Focus on Your Purpose, Not Your Past

Like the Apostle Paul, maybe you have a lot to forget, too. Aren't you ready? Does holding on to a failure

or a wrong help you? Does it accomplish anything?
Does it make you a better person? Can it change the
past?

No, holding on to past terrors or hurts, fears and
frustration doesn't do anything good. In fact, it does
harm. It can paralyze you from moving on; it can fill
you with bitterness and doubt. It can sink your self-
image. The father who was never there for his kids
will never be able to build a new relationship with
them till he believes he has love, not loathing, to give.
The doctor who misdiagnosed one patient can never
heal another until he chooses to learn from his mistake and try again.

Pressing forward means changing your focus from
you—all you did or didn't do—and focusing on your
purpose and what you are meant to do. It means taking God at his Word that he wants to do a new thing
for you. It means believing he cares for you, always
has, and always will. It means that instead of hanging
on to your past, you hang on to his promise that there
is absolutely nothing that can separate you from his
love. Not your past, not your present.[3]

Like Paul, then, we must forget what is behind and
strive for what is ahead. You must not focus on your
past, but on your purpose.

Does that mean losing all memory? No, forgetting
isn't necessarily erasing from your mind what's happened to you, but leaving things behind as done with

and settled. God promises you can do that. He says: *You can't change the past, but you can leave it behind recognizing that in my eyes the past is done with and settled.*[4]

Six Things to Forget So You Can Move Forward

If you think that's too hard, think about not doing so. If you are holding on to the past, you are essentially shackled. You are lugging around a heavy ball and chain.

Isn't that ridiculous? It not only looks bad because balls never really were in style, and chains are so last year. Dragging around a heavy ball and chain will wear you out, bring you down, keep you stuck in a very small place. A ball and chain tethers you, meaning you'll get nowhere fast. A ball and chain will force you to struggle more and work harder for less result; they will keep you from doing the exciting things God has for you to do. A ball and chain imprison you in so many ways, but there are six links in that chain that when broken can release you from that leaden ball:

1. Let go of guilt

A few years ago, I was eating lunch the day before I had plans to go on a trip to speak at a conference. Our then seven-year-old son, Christopher, asked in a matter-of-fact tone, "Why do you have to go on a trip without us?"

"Well," I replied, "a friend asked me to speak at her conference."

"Well," he said in a stronger tone, "you could have said no!"

I could literally feel the guilt wash over me. I began to explain to Christopher that I would be gone only two days (*two days!* splash) and I would be helping people (*and not my family!* splash, splash).

Christopher was quiet and finished his meal.

That seemed to satisfy him. I thought: *I explained! I did well! Yay me! He understands.*

When my son got up, he looked me square in the eyes and said, "You still could have said no!" (Big tsunami wave splashing here.)

Especially as a mother, I really have to resist the temptation to feel guilty. (If you don't watch it, motherhood can even make you feel guilty for feeling guilty!) It's too easy to allow myself to take a long guilt trip: *Why did I spend so much time studying today instead of more time with the girls?* (Now we're over the border.) *Why did I let myself get so irritated with the kids today?* (Now we're across the globe!)

Any one of us can take a guilt trip for any number of reasons. If we aren't careful, we will carry around guilt because of our weaknesses and shortcomings. We'll compare ourselves to other people, feeling as if we will never measure up. Such guilt is self-imposed. You find fault in yourself or blame and shame. You practice self-reproach. You hang on to that bad feeling that says you did all the wrong things or that you are inherently bad—and that says it all, because guilt doesn't make anyone feel good. Rather, it makes you feel insecure, less confident, inadequate, and unfit. It gnaws at you and steals your joy. It keeps you from enjoying today.

TO HELP YOU MORE

Walk Away from the Crutches

Letting go can be tough. But sometimes we are the ones who make it toughest—often without even realizing it. We hold on to things for dear life. We think these things help us get around, even get through a day. Actually they cripple us. They keep us from reaching our destiny. I'm talking about things like...

- **addictions**, everything from the usual suspects that people talk about, like drugs and alcohol, to the not-so-usually-mentioned food and television.
- **low-self esteem**, choosing to believe all the things we can't do instead of what God can do through us.
- **negative self-talk,** like how we tell ourselves that we can never do better or do more and that things are impossible.

Too often we make excuses for ourselves, too. We become consumed with the things, past or present, that don't matter. We let these things take our attention from what God has in mind for us. We are just like Peter in the Bible.

Remember the story (in Luke 5:1-11) of how Jesus wanted to bless Peter? Jesus asked to use Peter's boat to launch into deep waters so he could do something special for his fisherman friend.

Peter responds with all kinds of excuses: My partners and I have been working all night. We're tired. Not only that, we never even caught one fish.

Then Peter realizes these are crutches and they

aren't going to get him anywhere, at least not to the great place Jesus has for him. He throws down his crutches. "Okay," he tells Jesus, "because you say so I will launch my nets in the deep waters."

That was exactly what Jesus was waiting to hear. Because when we say, "All right, Lord, let's go," he takes us into the deep, the rich, the *more* of life he's had in store for us all along. For Peter, he filled those nets with so many fish they sagged and began to break.

Peter not only threw away his crutches that day, but in his journey to believe, he was shown that with Jesus he could walk on water. But that is another story...

We can put the brakes on guilt trips, though. That day Christopher told me I could have said no, I knew I had a choice to make. Was I going to take the guilt or let it go?

That day, I chose to let it go. I wouldn't have always done that, but I am learning that guilt steals from me. It sinks me in an ocean of bad feeling till I can do nothing but swim around in the frustration of my own making. That does nothing for anyone and only keeps me from enjoying my life.

Sometimes we have to choose to let go of guilt on a

daily basis. That means, situation by situation, choice by choice, learning to say: *I cannot please every person. I cannot help everyone. I cannot do everything people want me to do. I am not a superhero.*

I recently saw a funny quote about this: "I can only please one person per day. Today is not your day. Tomorrow doesn't look very good, either!"[5]

Doesn't it feel good to know you don't have to save the world or even your little corner of it. Whew! Relief! We can refuse to feel guilty for what we cannot do. We don't have to be perfect, just progressing. We are free to focus on our relationship with God and others.

2. Let go of childhood pain

Our good family friend, Joyce Meyer, tells how for many years as she was growing up, and in her own home, she was sexually abused. The horror is unimaginable. For years, Joyce wrestled with all kinds of physical, emotional, and spiritual issues. She felt intensely angry. She struggled. The issues began to control her . . . until she decided to let them go.

That is exactly how she describes it, too: she made a decision; she chose to let go of the anger and these issues. The freedom in that didn't come overnight. Over time, God transformed her into a beautiful and powerful minister who is influencing the world with his good news. But the decision took one moment.

Sadly, there is a world of people facing issues like Joyce. They've grown up in dysfunctional homes and negative environments. Yet dysfunction is not rare and is nothing new. It began with the very first family mentioned in the Bible. Adam and Eve's son, Cain, killed his brother, Abel.[6] Rebecca greatly favored one son, Jacob, over his twin brother, Esau.[7] Moses's siblings had a problem with his wife, who was from a different ethnic background.[8] King David's son raped his stepsister Tamar.[9]

I could go on, but I won't.

Maybe you are one of many who suffered as a child because of divorce, anger, poverty, abuse, incest, or an addiction that controlled your family. My heart goes out to you. More than that, God is full of compassion for you. Many people blame God for their pain, but the truth is he desires to take you into his loving arms and restore what people have stolen from you. He can heal the hurt, restore dignity, and actually use you to help make this world better.

Does that seem impossible? With God all things are possible. Ask Reggie, if you doubt.

Reggie grew up with a dad who struggled with alcoholism and drugs. Reggie's mom had died from a brain tumor when she was only twenty-five. Her father became addicted to heroin, and many nights didn't even come home. By nine years old, young Reggie began using drugs herself.

Late one night, her father came home, put her in the car, and dropped Reggie off at her grandmother's small apartment. He drove away, never to be involved in her life again.

At age fifteen, Reggie tried to attend high school, but she was too tired, too drunk, and too old in spirit for a normal high school life. She dropped out and found a home in bars and clubs by working in them for the next fifteen years. Daily drinking was now part of her lifestyle.

As she drank more and more, Reggie lost job after job. She couldn't stop. On her twenty-fifth birthday, she walked into her first Alcoholics Anonymous (AA) meeting and became sober for the first time in a couple decades. She began to learn about God and his promises to always love. Unfortunately her sobriety did not last because she kept turning to alcohol, haunted by her ugly childhood and hard past.

In desperation, she looked for God in a local church and found him and loving people seeking him too. At thirty-three years old, her life started to turn around again.

She could have kept turning to alcohol, but God kept showing up and promising so much more. Today Reggie is living proof of the more God has in mind. He helped her build a new life—and birth a new ministry that shares God's amazing grace with others.

What happened for Reggie can happen for you. Reggie realized God was greater than her negative up-bringing. She chose to believe in his power over her past. Letting go of that past didn't mean for Reggie, any more than it meant for Joyce, that you let peo-ple off the hook, that you minimize the pain. Letting go means deciding to free *yourself* to be who God cre-ated you to be. It means saying, *I refuse to let someone or some event determine my identity and self-worth.* It means your negative upbringing does not disqualify you from living a blessed, fulfilling life.

It means joy can be yours.

3. Let go of regret

I saw a sitcom not long ago where a young girl was hitting herself over the head with a soft bat all the time saying, "Why are you hitting yourself?" *Bam!* "Why are you hitting yourself?" *Bam!*

That is such a picture of regret, exactly what we do to ourselves when we indulge in regret. We inflict unnecessary pain upon ourselves. We choose turmoil and pain in the mind. We keep looking back at what might have been.

If only I would have done things different.

If only I had been a better mother.

If only I would have made better decisions.

We must come to the place where we accept the fact that we cannot go back and change our decisions and our actions.

There are better things we can do: We can let it go. We can let the past be the past once and for all. We can learn from our mistakes and live better.

As my brother Joel says, "Quit looking in your rearview mirror all the time." Instead, focus on how to improve yourself and make better decisions today.

Look to God instead of yourself and be encouraged, because God is the God of another chance. He believes in new beginnings. His mercies are new every morning. Remember his promise? *Do you perceive it? I will do a new thing!*

4. Let go of negative words people have spoken over you

I was in an elevator a few years ago with a mother and her young daughter. The little girl was just being a little girl, very energetic and excited. She wanted to push the buttons herself, but mistakenly pushed the wrong button. To my amazement, the mother scolded her and called her stupid.

I wanted to pick up that girl and say loudly: "You are not stupid. You are an incredible person and God has great plans for you."

That mother's words broke my heart. Can you imagine what it did to her daughter? I still think about that incident and feel sad. If a person will disgrace her child in public, I couldn't imagine what happened in the privacy of their home.

People can be so cruel with their words:

"You'll never amount to anything."

"You never do anything right."

"You aren't very bright, are you?"

"You are not a good wife."

These are lies that are hard to forget. They sink deep into our innermost being like a quarter going down the gumball machine:

Clink. *I'm stupid.*

Clink. *I'm worthless.*

Clink. *I'll never amount to anything.*

It's so easy to replay these negative words over and over in your mind, and the more you replay them the more you believe them, and the more the negative ideas become part of who you are.

But you must know today that the person who spoke negative words over you did not speak the truth. You are not what people say about you. You are God's creation and what He says is the truth. He says:

You are an incredible person, full of greatness.

You are valuable.

You have a beautiful mind, one of a kind.

You are gifted like no other.

Put that in your think tank! Replay that over and over again until you believe it and begin to act like it.

5. *Let go of little offenses*

Little hurts can become big hurts if we do not deal with them correctly. Many times we hold on to little things that people say and do, knowingly or unknowingly, that hurt our feelings. On a scale of one to ten, they are low, definitely not life shattering.

I think women tend to be more sensitive about the little things:

"Did you see the way Nancy looked at me today?"

"Sue didn't invite me to her party."

"My husband didn't even notice my new hairdo!"

If you want your husband to notice your new hairstyle, you've got to tell him you got one! That's a no-brainer!

Don't allow petty things to become a source of strife in your relationships. The Bible says: "Love believes the best of every person."[10] Give people the benefit of the doubt. Believe that they had no intention of offending you. We can make mountains out of molehills over little issues that don't really matter. Let go of the offenses and choose peace over strife.

6. *Let go of unforgiveness and bitterness*

I've been asked many times what to do when you've been hurt and are angry toward people who truly mistreated you. I've asked myself this many times, too. I had to forgive my ex-husband for wanting a divorce that to this day I don't understand. I've had to forgive a faceless, nameless person who sent a mail bomb intended to harm, even kill, my father and leaving me scarred. I've struggled so often with this question of how to forgive and let go—both for myself and others.

The truth is that if we do not find a way to forgive, bitterness will grow and become like trash in our lives. It will eventually decompose into a toxic poison that eats at you and kills your heart and spirit bit by bit.

Something amazing happens inside of you, however, when you let go of the hurt or anger, the bitterness and unforgiveness. There's a proverb that says, "The merciful man does good to his own soul."[11] When you forgive and let it go, you free yourself from that toxic poison. You find a release that allows God to bless you and promote you in a greater way. That's because the act of forgiveness isn't simply about helping someone who harmed you. It's about helping yourself.

Corrie ten Boom tells how she and her sister, Betsie, were placed in a Nazi concentration camp for hiding Jews in their home during World War II. They were terribly mistreated. Betsie died in the camp. Corrie survived, her faith in God intact, and became a sought-after speaker.

One day, she was in a little church in Munich telling

about God's great mercy and forgiveness.[12] At the end of the service, a man in a gray overcoat began to approach Corrie. Something about his walk toward her made her pause. Then she realized what it was: he was one of the cruel guards during her imprisonment. "It came back with a rush: the huge room with its harsh overhead lights, the pathetic pile of dresses and shoes in the center of the floor, the shame of walking naked past this man. I could see my sister's frail form ahead of me, ribs sharp beneath the parchment skin."[13] Corrie stood frozen as the guard approached.

"You mentioned you were in Ravensbruck Camp," he said when he stood before her. "I was a guard there, but since that time, I have become a Christian. I know that God has forgiven me, but I ask you to forgive me, too."

Corrie was speechless. "I remembered the slow terrible death of my sister in that place," she said, "and I, who had been forgiven over and over, could not forgive."

The man held out his hand to her, and in that moment she thought, *Forgiveness is not an emotion. It is an act of the will, and the will can function in spite of the temperature of the heart.* But she did not want to grasp that man's hand. Silently, she prayed: Jesus, help me!

And she thrust her hand into his.

"I forgive you, brother, with all my heart!" she said.

For a moment the former guard and the former prisoner grasped one another's hands. It was a moment that changed both their lives.

"I had never known God's love so intensely as I did then," Corrie said. "It was not my love—it was the power of the Holy Spirit who helped me forgive."

> *Corrie ten Boom thought,*
> **Forgiveness is not an emotion. It is an act of the will, and the will can function in spite of the temperature of the heart.**

How to Let Go

Whether you need to forgive someone else or forgive yourself to move on from your past, there is an important thing God wants you to know: he loves the forgiving heart and will give you the power to walk it out.

In fact, he will help you right here, right now. Letting go of the hurt, the bitterness, and anger begins with a decision, not a feeling. As Corrie told herself before grasping that guard's hand, forgiveness and letting go is an act of the will. You choose to forgive not because of what you will do for the other person but because it is the best thing for you.

Choosing to forgive someone does not necessarily make those who hurt you right. It doesn't even mean that your relationship will be mended or restored. But the choice does bring healing and restoration into your life and, many times, into the relationship itself.

Like in the worst possible house fire, Corrie lost her most precious possessions because of the stand she took for humanity. Corrie lost her entire family: her father, Casper; brother, Willem; nephew, Christian; and her beloved sister, Betsie. All Corrie had left after her release from Ravensbruck was ashes of what once was a happy life. She could have sat in those ashes, spent the rest of her days grieving such irrevocable losses. She could have held onto the pain and sorrow until it paralyzed her.

Instead, Corrie chose to hand the ashes to God. They were too much to carry anyway, she said. As she handed over those precious remains, she let God pick up the leftover pieces of her life, and she took them around the world, as she traveled and told, simply, of God's love and forgiveness—and she kept telling of it until he made it more real to her than she could have imagined. And it all began with a choice to let go.

Of course, once you make that choice to let go, some other choices will follow:

- **The choice to not dwell on the offense.** Don't push the rewind button and replay the offense over and over in your mind. When you do that, it stirs up the hurt and anger again. Instead, when you think about the person, do what the Bible says to do—pray for them.

- **The choice to not talk about an offender in a negative way.** Listen to your words. Are they angry and unforgiving? Or are they merciful? I heard someone say this and I really believe it because I have experienced it: You know you have forgiven and you have let it go when you think about that person and you don't get angry and you don't talk negatively about them.

- When you choose to forgive someone, you are choosing to show mercy, just like God does for us time and time again. Mercy is simply undeserved favor. Jesus said, "Freely you have received, freely give and blessed are the merciful, for they will be shown mercy."[14] We have to realize that if we want mercy in the future, then we need to be merciful to others today.

- *If you are carrying hurt, ask God to heal your broken heart.* You don't have to carry around that emotional pain all your life. You just have to let go of the hurt so God can heal you. The Bible says God heals the brokenhearted and binds up our wounds.[15] Corrie ten Boom would tell you God truly does heal the brokenhearted—and so would that guard who shook her hand. Your maker is in the mending business, and he loves nothing more than to restore the broken heart.

The Beauty of Letting Go

There's no doubt that some things are easier to let go of than others. For me, standing in the ashes, the sooty and soaked rooms left by the house fire that summer of 1984, there was definitely some sadness and uncertainty. But choosing not to stay in that place emotionally freed me from frustration and further sadness.

In fact, choosing to look ahead rather than back, allowed us to find some joy in the midst of what was terrible. During the reconstruction, we lived in a hotel suite, which turned out to be fun. After all, what teenagers don't like having beds made and bathrooms cleaned for them, guilt free? What a life—like being on a vacation.

When all was said and done, our insurance came through for us and our home was restored beautifully. It was almost like coming home to a brand-new house.

Our very souls are like that in the fires of life. Things will happen to make us feel burned alive, left in ashes, drowned in an ocean of sadness and loss. It's so tempting to wish for what was comfortable or familiar or loved before the fires of life. But when we release the past and grab hold of hope, we will see how God keeps his promises. We'll see how his promises are true. God will turn your mourning into dancing, and your sorrow into joy. He will give you beauty for your ashes.[16]

God longs to do something new. He wants you to move on toward your destiny—and to move mountains. He is ready to give the guilt-ridden new freedom to enjoy. He waits to give to sinners both forgiveness and another chance. To the sorrowful, he gives joy. To Reggie, he gave a new beginning; to Corrie, the power to forgive.

There is no telling what God has in store for you when you choose to let go, but one thing is sure: It will be amazing, beautiful, new.

Do you perceive it?

9

Finding More
When You've Been Labeled

*Because You're Made to Rise
above Others' Expectations*

~

I've struggled most of my life to weigh even ninety-five pounds. Today this is not a problem for me, but until ten years ago it seemed a huge challenge. I know many women think it would be great to be so thin, but when you can't seem to be anything but bony it's not great at all. What girl wants to be scrawny looking?

For one thing, our family was very athletic, except for me. Probably because of my early illness, I was never drawn to sports. My brothers and sisters competed in everything, and I enjoyed attending their games and watching my sisters as cheerleaders. But I seemed to always be the last in the physical education activities, especially running. The one sport I did all right in was dodgeball, and that was because I was so skinny that my classmates couldn't target me very well with the ball! And my most athletic activity was joining the school pep squad with my friend, Betsy.

Meanwhile, though, my classmates, and even my siblings, teased me about my lack of athletic ability and my scrawny girlhood. Believe me, I've heard all of the skinny jokes you can think of...

"You are so skinny, I bet you have to jump around in the shower to get wet."

"When you turn sideways, you disappear."

One of the worst things that the school boys called me was Olive Oyl.

Did you ever watch the cartoon *Popeye*? Well, Olive Oyl was the cartoon stick figure, the thin-as-a-toothpick-girl that Popeye and his archrival Brutus both loved. She was scrawny and skinny and plain looking. Skinny might be in today, but not back then. So being called Olive Oyl was not only hurtful, but an insult.

Olive Oyl.

How that label hurt—and stuck.

For years I had that negative picture in my mind: that I was too plain and too skinny. You know how cruel kids can be, but I learned to laugh with them. Yet deep down that label chiseled away at my self-esteem. I believed I was not acceptable because I didn't look like the other girls. I mean we women like to have some curves on us, don't we? And I was just a stick. I used to dress to make myself look a little bigger. I always layered my clothes, and I was really glad when shoulder pads came into style. I could use a little padding here and there.

Then I realized that I had allowed those negative words to not only affect the way I dressed, but to totally control how I thought of myself and even behaved. I accepted the labels others gave me. I not only accepted them but believed them.

Don't Believe Everything You Hear

Has anyone ever tried to label you? Have they told you what you cannot do and what you cannot be?

Sometimes we allow what people say to hold us back. They try to label us and we allow them to do so. We buy into their words spoken over us. We let that keep us from fulfilling our potential. Other times we are guilty of labeling ourselves all on our own.

Have you done that? Are you sure? I hear people say things like this all the time: "My life stinks." "I hate my job." "If I was better looking, I would get more breaks in life."

This is what we do. We say things that keep us from doing and being what God made us to do and be, things that hold us back. We put labels all over our life.

For years I accepted the OLIVE OYL label that one thoughtless schoolboy threw at me one day and repeated, and then others repeated over the years, even myself. Some of you have put labels on your life: LOSER. QUITTER. ALWAYS LATE. UGLY. STUPID. BORING. NO GOOD. SELFISH.

When you say those things, you steal your destiny. You hold yourself back from fulfilling the purpose you are meant for. Don't let anyone but God determine your destiny for you.

TO HELP YOU MORE

Dwell on What Is Right with You

You can focus on something that you or someone else says is wrong with you. But that will do nothing except keep you stuck, feeling bad about yourself, worthless. But what if you chose to think on what is right with you, how God made you just as he wanted, just as he needed, for you to do the great things he has in mind for you?

There is a story in the Bible of a man named Haman who was faced with that choice.

Haman chose to believe what others said, and in so doing he set his life on the path to destruction. Did you know that you can set your life on the path to victory or destruction by your own choices?

Haman completely overreacted to this one negative thing in his life—that another man, Mordecai, wouldn't bow down to him. This hurt Haman's pride. He must have thought Mordecai was essentially saying (which he was): "You are not worthy of my adoration."

Haman had grander ideas of himself than were actually true. He was wealthy, and he felt entitled. One day, he was bragging about his life to his wife and friends, bragging about all his wealth and sons and honors, and he realized a truth: things didn't make him special. He wasn't so much the great guy he thought, if Mordecai wouldn't bow to him.

Haman thought about Mordecai day and night, until he allowed anger to fill his heart. He wanted revenge. But he didn't want it just on Mordecai. That wasn't enough. He wanted it on all Mordecai's people. He decided to get rid of all the Jews. He was very manipulative and convinced the King that all of the Jews were in rebellion to him. So the King issued a decree to eliminate all the Jews in Persia.

What Haman didn't know was that Queen Esther, the woman the King loved so much and who was Mordecai's relative, was also a Jew.

Poor Haman. He chose to dwell on all the

wrong things—what he thought would define his destiny, but instead defined his doom. He listened to himself and tried to orchestrate what he thought should be happening in his life, instead of listening to God.

A lot of us are like Haman. We can only see and hear the negative things in life. But we have a choice. We can allow negative circumstances or comments, what one person does or says to us, to destroy our peace and joy.

But nothing is worth that.

Instead, if we dwell on the good things, on God, he will make a way for us. He will show us things that are greater.

Maybe you always wanted to teach math, but someone told you once only Harvard scholars should do that, and you made it only to community college. Are you going to let that comment keep you from pursuing your dream? Or maybe you love to garden and grow flowers and secretly dreamed of opening a florist shop. But someone told you only those with pure business savvy should open a shop. Are you going to waste your green thumb from bringing beauty to others because of a careless comment someone made once?

My brother, Joel, could have listened to the naysayers when he stepped in to pastor Lakewood. Some theologians even predicted in the *Houston Chronicle* that Lakewood would never succeed under his leadership because he had never preached before or attended seminary. They also said that our father was such a powerful, charismatic leader that it would be a mistake for him to try to follow in his dad's footsteps. But I admire how Joel chose to believe what God said about him instead of what others said. Don't expect other people to understand the dreams God has put in your heart, the destiny he's prepared for you to step into.

Don't Buy the Bad Others Say about You

Life will always try to make you believe the worst about yourself. What happened to me in childhood happened to my friend Damon in a more dramatic way. Before even his teenage years, Damon grew up believing he was limited and labeled.

Things began to spin out of control for Damon when he was twelve years old. His father left his mother, and it shattered him. Knowing that his father always had a loaded gun in his bedroom, Damon decided one day to take his life. Thoughts of hopelessness and desperation plagued him as he put the gun to his head. His hand trembled as he mustered the nerve to pull the trigger. Click. Damon heard the trigger release...but realized he was still alive. Even though his father's gun was fully loaded, it didn't fire.

Damon's mother, discovering her son's suicide attempt, knew it was a miracle the gun hadn't gone off. Tears streaming down her face, she said, "Damon, God has a plan for your life and don't ever forget it."

For a while, though, Damon did forget. He grew angry at the hopelessness and became rebellious. He struggled with everything and everyone. He was labeled a troublemaker, and his high school principal told him that he would be in prison by the time he was eighteen. Another adult, who overheard Damon cursing at a sporting event, repeated that prediction: "You will be institutionalized by the time you're eighteen."

Damon's rebellious ways led him to join racial hate groups, feeding his anger and rebellious ways. At a party one night, a fight broke out and bullets began to fly. Damon fired shots, hitting two people. People were screaming as police were called to the scene. Hearing the approaching sirens, Damon fled by jumping into the trunk of a friend's car. The friend sped away and dropped Damon off in the woods, as helicopters swirled overhead looking for suspects.

Lying there alone in the dark woods, being hunted down, Damon thought of all the labels put on him: BAD BOY. WOULD-BE CRIMINAL. DROPOUT. HATER.

His current circumstances seemed to suddenly unfold in slow motion. *How,* he thought, *did I get here?*

Then he remembered what his mother told him: "Damon, God has a plan for your life."

He threw a prayer up to Heaven: "God, if you can get me out of this hell that I am in, I will serve you for the rest of my life."

He believed God's promise of a plan and wanted to make a promise back to God—and God took him up on it.

After praying, Damon said the fear he was feeling, the desperation, melted away. A peace he had never known before suddenly filled all the places where anger, hurt, and frustration had been. Lying there in the dark for a while, Damon thought about God, then made his way home. He was never questioned about the incident, even though others, including his then girlfriend, were picked up by police for questioning. Damon got serious about the promise he had made in the woods. He decided to relabel himself. He went back to school to complete his education. LEARNER. He began to attend a great church and eventually a Bible School for young adults. GOOD MAN. He dedicated himself to helping troubled youth and inmates. LOVER OF GOD AND PEOPLE. He offered hope to others who were being negatively labeled, too, warning of the dangers of wrong associations. CRIME PREVENTER.

You can choose to believe negative words spoken by others about you, Damon learned, or you can choose to believe God.

You are not a loser. *You are a winner.*

You are not worthless. *You are valuable.*

You are not a good-for-nothing. *You offer something unique and incredible to this world.*

You are not destined for dead ends or death row. *Your life is worth living—and living richly, abundantly, without limits.*

If you will just continue to walk forward, toward positive things for yourself and others, you will step into God's great plan for your life. God is greater than any boyfriend or girlfriend problems, a broken home, drug addictions, suicidal thoughts, or hopeless feelings. As he did for Damon, God will get you out of dark places, out of the woods in life and help you re-label yourself as he sees you.

Will You Ask to Be Relabeled?

But are you ready for a new identity? I love the story in the Bible of a man named Bartimaeus because he wanted to be known as God saw him and Bart wouldn't listen to what others said about his destiny.[1] He wouldn't take no for an answer to his cries for a new identity, either. Bartimaeus was sitting by the roadside begging for money in the city of Jericho, when he heard that Jesus was coming through town.

Bartimaeus was so excited. He began to shout loudly, over and over, "Jesus, have mercy on me." He wanted to get Jesus's attention. He did not want to miss his moment, but his shouting was annoying the people around him. His radical faith was too much for them. The people scolded Bartimaeus and told him to be quiet.

They put that label on him: LOUD. ANNOYING. They didn't understand Bartimaeus's dream at all. They didn't have any sympathy for his plight. Can you imagine that? You would have thought they would have compassion on him and helped him. He was blind and couldn't get to Jesus without help. These people knew Jesus could heal him. They had just seen Jesus perform such miracles. But instead of helping Bartimaeus, they told him to be quiet.

I like how Bartimaeus wouldn't take no for an answer. The people's response to him just made him all the more determined. The Bible says Bartimaeus shouted all the more, all the louder, "Jesus, have mercy on me!"

And all of a sudden, Jesus stopped and said: *I hear the cry of faith. I hear somebody reaching for their destiny. I hear someone who refuses to take no for an answer. Bring Bartimaeus to me!*

Now that Bartimaeus had Jesus's attention, the people around him had a different attitude. They said: *Cheer up, Bart. Jesus is calling for you. Let me help you get to Jesus. Oh, and Jesus, look what I did.*

A lot of people will try to talk you out of things, but when you reach your destiny, they will be knocking at your door. They will act like your work or your vision was their idea. Too many of us are fickle too much of the time. That's why you have to ignore the labels people give you and follow what you hear God telling you. Listen to what he says you are and can do.

This takes determination. It requires unwavering faith in what God says, not other people. Bartimaeus cried out to Jesus until he got his attention. Jesus healed Bartimaeus and commended him for such unwavering faith. Sometimes we give up too easily. We give in to the words people speak over us or we speak over ourselves. Be determined to reach your destiny. When people try to stop you with their words, just be more determined than ever. They don't have that power to keep you from what God has in store, unless you give that power to them.

Remove the Negative Labels

Of course that can be easier said than done. There will always be people who doubt that you are more than what they think. We live in a world of people that plant such thoughts every day, and we often are the ones who water and grow those thoughts. Even the prophets of old struggled with this.

Jeremiah was a young man when God first called him to do great things with his life. God said, "Before I shaped you in the womb, I knew all about you. Before you saw the light of day, I had holy plans for you: A prophet to the nations—that's what I had in mind for you."[2]

TO HELP YOU MORE

Jesus Can Give You a New Label

He did that for Peter, a fisherman who accepted Jesus's invitation to follow him. Before they met, Peter was known as Simon, a rough fisherman who needed a lot of work on his character and relationships. You see, Peter was labeled: HOT-HEAD, IMPULSIVE, HEADSTRONG. He rubbed people the wrong way, shot off his mouth, did things his own way even when it caused hurt to himself.

Jesus didn't see those labels, though. He didn't see Peter as he was in the present. Jesus saw Peter as God had made him to be, and as Peter was going to be when he got through with him. Jesus labeled Peter: PASSIONATE, DETERMINED, STRONG.

Jesus told Peter, "You are Simon, son of John. But you will be called Cephas, which means Peter" (John 1:42). Jesus was saying: *You are my rock. Your life may be like sifting sand now, but when I get ahold of you then you're going to be solid as a rock.*

That's what Jesus does for us. He takes who we are and embraces us. He loves how God made us, and he sees what is best and calls that out of us, ever shaping and sharpening our best qualities like the potter does with the clay to create something beautiful and enduring.

Think about words that describe you. Write them down. Tuck the list in your Bible or tape it someplace you'll see it. Pray over these labels and how God can turn anything negative to a positive. Pray to and ask God to relabel you and give you a new name.

God promises to do that. "I will give you a white stone with a new name on it," he says (Revelation 2:17). Meditate upon what name your stone will bear.

Wow. God had big plans for Jeremiah, plans that began before he was even born. But Jeremiah struggled to believe it. He had so many self-imposed labels: TOO YOUNG. POOR SPEAKER. NOT GOOD ENOUGH. He opened his mouth and got in trouble. He told God: *Hold it, Master and God! Look at me. I don't know anything. I'm only a boy!*

If only Jeremiah had known, like we should know, when God speaks, learn to shut up and listen because God answers: "Do not say, 'I am only a child.' You must go to everyone I send you to and say whatever I command you."[3] God was serious because he had a destiny for Jeremiah. God was adamant about it, too. He said: *Do not speak those words over your life. I created you, and I know what you are capable of doing. If you were too young, don't you think I would know it?*

God doesn't want you to put a negative label on yourself. He is saying to you: *Stop saying those negative things. It's time to remove the labels. Take the limits off of yourself. When you do, you will be surprised at what you find.*

Look for Positive Labels

Fortunately, I had parents that spoke positive words of encouragement to me. They rejected others' labels of what we could not do, beginning with the doctors at my birth—the doctors who said I would never walk or develop well and probably never lead a re-motely normal life.

Thank goodness. Because of their belief in me and not the labels, I have surprised everyone. I walk just fine, and I don't know if my life has been normal or not, but I'm grateful they encouraged me to reject such labels, too.

In fact, my mother, Dodie, says often, "Make your words sweet because you may have to eat them one day."

The sweet words she used for my brothers and sisters and I were definitely the right stuff. Every morning as we hurried out the door to school, she prayed over me (and each of us specifically): "Thank you, Father, that Lisa is blessed and that you surround her with your favor. The angels of God watch over her. No harm, accidents, or broken bones will come near her." Then she would say, "Now go get on the bus!"

That was just a normal part of our morning schedule—and it is amazing how far an encouraging word can go. Our mother's words carried us through sickness, and none of us ever broke a bone.

Our daddy was equally generous in speaking good words over us. He called us blessings all the time. People would say to him, "Isn't it hard raising all those children?"

"No," he would respond. "They are gifts from God and we enjoy them!"

When I heard that, I would stand a little taller.

Others would say, "Just wait until they become teenagers—they will give you so much trouble."

But our father refused to put that label of TROUBLE on us. He would say, "I am not going to fear the teen years. We are going to enjoy every year because all of our children are blessings."

That, too, made me stand taller—and want to do better and be a blessing. His words raised the level of my self-esteem.

Each of us can do what my mother and father did for us. I like to think of this as using your verbal label gun—you know, those gadgets that let you type in words and produce stick-on labels. Well, I encourage you to get your imaginary label gun out and get busy! If you need to, change the labels on your life. Start speaking good words over your mate, your children, your friends.

A few years ago I was talking to a friend about her ideas for her ladies' meetings, and I was struck with her ingenuity. I said casually, "You are so creative! How do you think of all those things?"

It wasn't until recently that I learned what that meant to her. She told me that I was the first person to ever tell her that she was creative. At the time, she was in her late thirties and she had never really thought of herself in that way. But that one comment from the heart sparked something in her, and she realized that was one of her gifts that she has since allowed God to develop in her more.

It's amazing how far an encouraging word can go, how much more is in store for the person kind words are spoken to and about and for.

Certainly the words others speak, or that we utter, feed us with truth or untruth—and feed others, too. But I realize not everyone is surrounded by such positive, faithful people like I was with my parents.

A man named Jabez wasn't.

The Labeling of Jabez

Strange name, Jabez, right? Even in Bible times, Jabez's name was an oddity, almost as bad as Icabod. His mother gave him the name Jabez because it means "to make sorrowful, cause distress, and be in pain."

Ouch. If you thought your mama was bad, how would you like this mom? What a bitter woman for calling her son after the pain she had bearing him. Doesn't every woman experience some pain in childbirth?

What Jabez's mother did was project her hurt and bitterness onto her son. Many times that happens in life. Maybe it's happened to you. For Jabez, every time his mother called him by name, she was saying: *You make me sorrowful. I will never forget how much pain you caused me at birth.* She tried to label her son and shame him all his life.

I am intrigued by what is written about Jabez, whose story is almost hidden in a long list of genealogy of the Hebrew tribes.[4] The first chapter of 1 Chronicles begins listing the genealogy with Adam and then continues listing descendants through chapters two and three. But then you get to chapter four, and the author stops listing names and makes a few side comments that are arresting. For some reason, the writer determined, *I have to tell the story of Jabez. I can't just list his name.*

And that is what is amazing. By his very name, the label his mother meant for ill, Jabez becomes known for what God meant all along: something good.

TO HELP YOU MORE

Have You Ever Labeled Others?

Have you labeled someone else as LESS THAN, UNWORTHY, BAD, UNQUALIFIED? Each of us has judged someone else's worth at some time or another.

Jesus said, "Love your neighbor as you love yourself" (Luke 10:27). Until we learn to love and value ourselves as God does, we can't truly love others. As we begin to see the value that God places on us, then we begin to see the value of other people, too. When we recognize what God has done for each of us, we will be less critical and judgmental, and more merciful and loving.

God created each of us, and who are we to criticize or judge what he made and declares his workmanship, a masterpiece?

Beginning today, choose to be intentional about this. Think on what the Bible tells us: "For whatever point you judge others, you are condemning yourself, because you who pass judgment do the same things" (Romans 2:1).

Changing your thinking from being critical and judgmental requires simply this: Each time you catch yourself putting down others or yourself, stop. That's it. Tell yourself: *I'm not going to think this way. I'm not going to criticize God's workmanship.* Instead of something negative look for something positive to think or say.

This is living like Jesus said to do: To love others as yourself.

Jabez, the Bible tells us, was more honorable than his brothers.[5] His mother had named him Jabez, saying, "I gave birth to him in pain."

But Jabez prayed to God, "Oh that you would bless me and enlarge my territory! Let your hand be with me, and keep me from harm so that I will be free from pain."[6]

And God granted his request.

When Jabez reached out to the Lord, he was reaching for more! He refused to let his own mother label him and determine his destiny. Instead of living below his God-given potential, he determined to look for more in life. He asked big. He prayed a short but life-changing prayer. And he made four powerful requests of God that changed his destiny forever.

Pray Like Jabez for No Limits, No Labels

You can make the same requests Jabez made to change your life for good in every way.

1. Pray: "God, bless me!"

It doesn't matter what kind of a family or community you grew up in, you can break free from that pain and negative reputation and bondage. God has more for you, if you will only ask him for it. His Word reminds us of this very fact: you do not have because you do not ask God.[7] That's all Jabez did. He simply asked. He said: *I don't want to live a life of pain. I want to be different than my brothers and my mother! I know I am made for more than this! I want to live a blessed life!*[8]

And God answered. God blessed Jabez so that his destiny even reached our ears thousands of years later, and we're still talking about him today. God made his name beautiful, not one of sorrow, for it was through Jabez's lineage that the Bible tells us we got Jesus.

You don't need to repeat the bitter or ugly cycle of your parents or upbringing or community any more than Jabez did. And all you have to do to begin to break the cycle is ask, "God, bless me!" and wait and see what God will do.

2. Pray: *"God, enlarge me!"*

Jabez wanted more than his mother's loathing. Do you want more—more than what others say about you? Do you want to make a difference, do great things? Have you determined: *I am not settling for where I am today. I am ready, God, for you to do something new in me?* Then ask God like Jabez did. Cry out loud like Bartimaeus did:

Increase me!
Change me!
Transform me!
Use me!
Open doors for me!
Multiply me!

Enlarge my influence!

God's not just listening. He is loving, and both the story of Jabez and Bartimaeus show that he hears you and will make a way for you.

3. Pray: *"God, let your hand be with me!"*

Jabez didn't want to go anywhere without God's presence, favor, and blessing. That means he started looking for ways that God could be by his side, rather than his mother's words. He looked to God for leading rather than for a label of sorrow. He listened for God in his life rather than others.

You can do that. You can let go of the labels others would leave you with. You can take God's hand and he won't let go. He makes that promise.[9]

4. Pray: *"God, keep me from a life of trouble and pain!"*

Jabez determined: *I am not going to let my mother choose my destiny. I don't want to live a life of pain. I want to live for you, God! I want to be a blessing to other people.* He recognized the power of labels and how his mother tried to use that over him. He decided that his mother didn't have the authority to choose his destiny for him, and he didn't want to cause the pain he had experienced to anyone else.

Just recently I realized that I needed to let go of

some negative words that a person spoke over me years ago. This person was a well-meaning lady, but she spoke something negative about my future, and I didn't realize until much later that I was still holding on to what she said.

I was allowing this lady's words to affect my present life. Without knowing it, I had let her thoughts, however careless or well intended, take root in me. They were always in the back of my mind. I didn't hold anything against that lady, but her words stuck with me for twenty years. She had tried to place a limit on me, however unknowingly.

So I had to uproot those negative words. Like Jabez, I released them. I said: "I believe I have a good and a bright future! I release those negative words because they are not a part of my life or destiny." When I prayed to be released from the trouble and pain of those words, I experienced a freedom in my spirit.

God wants you to remove any negative label so you can be free to enjoy your life and fulfill your purpose. But, in addition to praying like Jabez, how do you do that?

See Yourself as God Does

God wants you to have a good self-image and feel

good about who you are. He created you and your destiny, and he has a great label waiting for you. God urges us to present our bodies as a living sacrifice, holy and pleasing to him, because this is our true and proper worship.[10]

Notice that God didn't say to present yourself to him, if you can preach, or if you have great talents, or if you're already labeled by others as AMAZING, GREAT, BEAUTIFUL.

No, the Bible says: *Present yourself to God and let God take it from there. Make yourself available to him, and what you can't do, he will.*

Doing this is an action that begins with the understanding and belief that God loves how he made you and he made you to do something great. The images you have of yourself affect your actions and reactions, your relationships, and every area of your life. That's why you need to build your self-image according to what God says, not others. God doesn't want you to go through life beat down and oppressed, thinking negative thoughts about...

- **your relationship with him,** because he wants you to know he has accepted and chosen you. He actually picked you out for himself.

- **your personality,** because he lovingly made you just the way you are—wonderfully. God gave you certain qualities and characteristics that no one else has quite like the combination in you, and he has plans just for you.

- **your physical appearance,** because your value and beauty aren't based on the outer body. Your worth is based on the inward person of the heart. Warmth and godliness come out of your spirit. That doesn't mean you don't take care of yourself or try to look your best, but focus most on what's inside.

- **your ability or lack of ability,** because God wants you to stand tall as his child, who is confident and secure in him. You may say, "I don't feel confident. I don't have ability." I understand. Sometimes I still get a little nervous when I get up to speak, feeling inadequate. In those moments I do what I know to work: I take a step in faith (you might call it a leap, a plunge!). I look for confidence that God is going to help me. What I learn anew, every time, is that if you don't step out in faith and do something, God can't help you, and you'll never know the thrill of finding out what he can do through you.

To start working out what these things mean in your everyday life, there are three things you can begin doing right now.

1. Listen to what you say about yourself

You can't control what other people say about you,

but you can control your own words. So many times we're our own worst labeler, and we trap ourselves by saying things like:

- "I don't like myself." The trap: if you don't like yourself, you begin to think other people must not like you, either.
- "I can't do anything right." The trap: if you think you do everything wrong, you lose confidence in yourself.
- "I'm not a beautiful person." The trap: if you think you're unattractive to other people, you begin to act like it, then believe it, and create false illusions of what is beautiful.

Such negative words and thinking will push you down into a spiral of darkness. The more negative things you say about yourself, the more you draw attention to yourself and your weaknesses. Before long, what you say becomes true and others begin to see you as weak, which you live up to—or down to.

Each of us has flaws, but we must learn to focus on our strengths. One of my friends used to always talk about her big nose. I thought she was beautiful, but she frequently talked about what she considered a flaw. She would say, "I hate my nose! It has a hump on it." I told her, "I don't even notice it! Quit thinking that." After pointing out her imperfect nose to me again and again, unfortunately I began to focus on it, too. I began to notice the hump. Too many times we complain about things that others don't even notice. So, shhh! Don't tell anyone and learn to shut down that bad voice in your own mind.

Really, her nose wasn't that big, but she drew attention to it because she voiced her insecurity over and over. I wouldn't have noticed her nose at all if she hadn't kept talking badly about it.

> *Each of us has flaws, but we must learn to focus on our strengths.*

What weaknesses, inabilities, and insecurities of yours do you talk about—to yourself or others?

If you can't speak anything positive over your own life, then speak what the Bible says about you. Did you know it speaks of you? It does! Look at this. The Bible says, "Let the weak say I am strong."[11] That means: Don't say what you feel and see on your own. Instead, say what God says about you:

- "I am God's child and I am blessed."[12]
- "I am gifted, talented, and smart."[13]
- "My beauty comes from the inside—from the hidden person of the heart."[14]
- "God loves me and values me. He has accepted me and I'm going to accept myself."[15]

You encourage or discourage yourself by what you say. You can raise or lower your self-esteem by your own words. So listen to what you are saying about yourself.

2. Don't compare yourself to other people

You'll never feel good about yourself as long as you look at other people and compare yourself: "I wish I was like that. I wish I could do that. I wish I could be a mother like she is. I wish I could have a business like he has. I wish I looked like she did."

No, if wishes were fishes that kind of talk would make you smell pretty bad! In other words: heaping wishes like that upon yourself is rotten. If God wanted you to be like someone else, he would have made you like they are. Instead, he made you—you! Unique! Special!

Sure, there are times we look at someone else and think: *What a great mom. What a great dad. What a great cook. How creative. How athletic.* And we wish we were that person. I do that. But I'm learning to stop and say to myself, *That is what makes them so special. I appreciate those strengths in them, but I have different strengths. I have a different personality and I'm going to be who God created me to be.*

Someone once said that they wished I preached more like Joel. When I heard that, the first thing I thought was, *I don't want to preach like Joel because I don't want to be an imitation of someone. I am an original.* Besides, Joel has his own unique style. In fact, each of my brothers and sisters preach, but we are all different in our style of communicating. Sure, there are similarities because we are from the same family, but God made each of us unique in our own way. If I am going to fulfill my potential, I have to be me—and you have to be you. God wants you to know: there is no one like you, and you alone are awesome and powerful. Just because you don't have some of the same strengths or gifts that someone else has doesn't mean there's something wrong with you. The most powerful you is the real you. Be genuine, authentic, and true to who God created you to be.

3. Recognize your own special qualities and gifts

God made you unique. He made you special. You may be musically inclined, but even Beethoven wasn't made just like you.

When I think on uniqueness, one of our volunteers at Lakewood Church comes to mind. She puts together the most amazing packets of information. She is blessed with natural gifts of organization. Not everybody has that gift, and she is using it just for us.

The Bible says that God has given each of you a gift from his great variety of spiritual gifts, and we are to use them well to serve one another.[16] Did you get that? You have received a gift, something other people don't have exactly as it is in you. "Do not neglect the gift that is in you," the Bible adds.[17]

The Ultimate Label

When you begin to not only see what your gifts are, but label yourself with them and use them, your life will be transformed. You will look back and think, *How could I have had such a poor self-image when God has done so much for me?* You'll wonder: *Why was it easier to see destiny and purpose in the lives of others and not myself?* You'll stop wearing those labels from childhood or teen years, the enemy's designer labels and your own self-talk that you're not good enough and will never be good enough. You'll start listening to God's labels for yourself. He is the Ultimate Designer. Talk about wearing designer labels! Wear God's:

CHOSEN.[18]

PRECIOUS.[19]

ONE OF A KIND.[20]

APPLE OF MY EYE.[21]

FAVORED.[22]

BLESSED.[23]

SUCCESSFUL.[24]

God tells us he wants to birth something new in our lives. He says: *From one man, I made every nation of men that they should inhabit the whole earth; and I determined the times set for you and the exact places where you should live. I did this so that you would seek me and perhaps reach out for me and find me, though I am not far from each one of you.*[25]

Did you hear that? God is near. He has his hand on you. He has placed you at the right time and place. He wants you to walk away from the pain of other people's labels and into the joy of his purpose for you. I remember the day I decided to choose what God says about me instead of living under all those old childhood OLIVE OYL labels. I decided since God saw me as his wonderful creation I would live like that, even if I was a little Olive Oyl–like. Hey, Popeye loved Olive. Others could, too! I was not going to let anyone steal my self-worth because of what some ignorant people said to me. Getting over the labels given us is that choice we each have to make. No one can do it for you.

When I was in Florence, Italy, with some friends, I found a ring that has a portrait of Olive Oyl. It is big and oval, and Olive's portrait is surrounded by rhinestones. She is even wearing diamond earrings! I love to wear this ring. Olive Oyl used to be a negative picture in my mind, but today she inspires me to be myself. This ring reminds me that no one is ever going to label me or control my destiny. And the truth is, when I look at Olive Oyl today, I think she's pretty cute.

And so does God. And he has a plan for her, for me, for you. His is a plan with no limits and only good labels of MINE and LOVED and PERFECT for you and for me.

10
Finding More When You Fail

*Because You're Made to Succeed
and to Encourage Success*

ɷ

Recently I was in a little town overlooking one of California's beautiful beaches. A group of ladies brought me there from a conference where I was scheduled to speak, and I wanted to get a group photo. I asked a man who happened to be walking by if he would mind taking the picture. He was happy to oblige us and we struck up a conversation.

When he found out that I was from Texas, he said, "I love that Joel Osteen in Houston!"

We smiled and I told him that Joel is my brother.

The man was elated. He beamed and told me, with joyful tears in his eyes, how Joel's encouraging messages helped him make it through a bout with cancer.

"Do you have a good church that you attend here?" I asked.

The man hung his head. "I am ashamed to go back to church," he said. "When I was going through chemotherapy, I went back on drugs."

My heart broke over the man's shame and state of being stuck by his relapse with drugs. He thought he was all washed up, like one of those beach stones, beaten and tossed by the waves onto the ocean shore. We hugged him, prayed with him, and assured him: "God loves you. He doesn't see you as a failure. He caused our paths to cross because he wants you to know that he believes in you. God sees someone he loves and wants to spend time with—forever."

As we arranged for the man to attend the church where I was speaking that weekend, I marveled at such an unexpected encounter. I was taking time away from what I thought was the real ministry of my weekend. This man was just passing by a group of ladies on his walk along the beach. But God loved this man so much that he wanted to encourage him. So God used me at the right place at the right time— more than 1,400 miles away from Houston.

The funny thing is, I thought I went to California to do my ministry in speaking at that conference, but God was looking out for one man who was hurting. Who's to say my greatest ministry wasn't in simply being there for that one person on the beach?

If you are that "one person" today, God is looking out for you, too. He will go out of his way to meet you where you are, to help you get moving in the right direction again. God always goes out of the way to help us. But when we fall, when we fail, why is it so hard to see that?

We Need Each Other

Shame gets a lot of the blame when it comes to reaching out to others out of failure. So many people are ashamed to ask for help. We think asking for help is an admission of being less than perfect. But we *are* less than perfect! We're *im*perfect! Why do we think we have to maintain any other façade? We are human, and the God who made us that way understands.

The Bible says that Jesus understands our weaknesses because he faced all of the same testings and temptations that we do, yet he never sinned.[1] I like the way the *Message* Bible words this: God is not out of touch with our reality, so let's walk right up to him and get what he is so ready to give. Take his mercy, accept his help.[2]

Isn't that beautiful? *Take his mercy, accept his help.* He offers us a compassionate hand. But how can we receive his help, unless we admit our faults and ask for that help?

When I think of the answer to this, I think of how Kevin and I first held our newborn twin girls in the hospital nursery when they were only one day old. One of the nurses on duty that day told us a precious story that I will always remember, a story about need.

The nurse said right after birth, it didn't seem that Caroline could be comforted. The nurses fed her, held her, and cared for her, but when they placed her in the incubator, she would cry. Continually. What on earth could be wrong? She was getting food. Her diaper was clean. She was warm and safe.

Finally, it dawned on this nurse what was wrong. Against hospital policy, the nurse placed Caroline with Catherine in her incubator so they could be together. Caroline never cried again. In fact, the girls locked arms and slept peacefully for the next three days.

How we need each other. Even little babies show us this most primal of needs. We were made for relationships. We need people in our lives to lock arms with us, encourage us, be there for us because we will fail. Every one of us will fail at something sometime. And when we are fallen we are at our most vulnerable. We are down. We have trouble getting up again. That's why it is important to get involved in a good local church with a pastor who cares for you. We also need to be the type of people who will encourage and support others in their time of need.

The Nature of Failure

We are each in the process of transformation, meaning as we grow our minds, bodies, and spirits, we make mistakes. That is part of growing: little falters, big falls. God doesn't expect us to be perfect, but he does expect us to learn and stretch, improve, and refuse to allow failure to defeat us. But first understand some truths about failure:

Failure may be a temporary detour, but it's not a dead end

Every person on the planet has experienced failure, but just because you fail doesn't mean you are a failure. If there is one thing I want you to understand about failure, it's that failure is never final. Failure is delay, not defeat—a detour, not a dead end. You are made to rise above failure and to be successful.

I like the way Paul J. Meyer, a businessman who went on to make millions, says this: "Ninety percent of all those who fail are not defeated. They simply quit."[3]

A dear friend of mine, Penny, could not have been happier when she and her husband began to pastor a great church in Texas. In high school, she was the popular cheerleader whom everyone loved. She brought the same enthusiasm into their newfound church. In her mind, she was a part of God's big party every Sunday, and all of her friends were coming. Why not? Life was intended to be celebrated, and life couldn't have been better.

Then things changed. Longtime friends left the church for no apparent reason. Penny felt rejected and forsaken. She tried reasoning with them, but to no avail. She began to wrestle with thoughts of failure, guilt, and regret: *Maybe I did something wrong. Maybe I'm not capable of undertaking such a task.*

She resigned herself to negative, untrue thoughts and found herself in bed, so depressed that she was unable to get up in the morning. She went from jumping out of bed on Sundays, excited to encourage and cheer her congregation, to having her mother prod her to dress and then drive her to church.

Symptoms of sickness began to overwhelm Penny's body, though the doctors could find nothing wrong with her. This went on for a year until one day Penny decided that enough was enough. She decided that she was not a failure and that just because a few friends walked out on her did not change the original plan God had for her life.

Penny might have stayed in bed, but day after day she chose to believe she was not made to fail but to fly, to soar, toward her destiny. Today Penny and her husband are living in that destiny. They lead a growing church in the middle of two inner-city apartment complexes in Angleton, Texas, and they are making a difference for people who need hope.

I believe that you have that same get-up-and-at-'em spirit as Penny, that you are not a quitter. The very fact that you are reading this book and interested in more in life is a sign that you want to be better to-morrow than you are today. With that spirit you will never fail, and God will get you where he means you to be.

Failure is an event, not a person

When I think of people who had to overcome failure, I think of Peter, one of Jesus's twelve disciples. But I don't think this is because Peter personifies failure. No one does. Failure is not what we are or who we be-come—it is an event or events in our lives that come and go. Failure is an event that people overcome.

Peter was such a person, and the kind of person most of us can understand—so relatable. He was rough around the edges, brash, a fisherman prone to anger easily and to say exactly what he thought and felt precisely when he felt it, no matter whose feelings were at stake. But Jesus saw great potential in Peter. In fact, Jesus believed in him so much that he gave him that name: Peter, which means "rock." When they met, Peter's name was Simon, but Jesus saw Peter's strength like a stone, and called him so.

That's so encouraging because Peter experienced so many personal failings, and yet that's not what God sees when he looks at any of us. He doesn't see FAIL-URE like a badge on a shirt or a name on a ball cap. When God looks at us, he sees our hearts and both what we are as well as what we are becoming. He sees the possibility in us, strength as strong as rock, the potential.

In Peter, he saw so many good things. For three years, Peter worked faithfully with Jesus. However, he also failed Jesus. Peter made all kinds of mistakes, some little and some big. One time, Peter didn't like what Jesus was saying, and he began to correct and rebuke Jesus. Can you imagine correcting Jesus? Another time, Peter got so angry that he cut off a man's ear. Jesus graciously healed the man, but that severing act showed a tremendous lack of self-control in Peter.

In spite of Peter's shortcomings, Jesus never gave up on him. Jesus loved Peter, and long before they met, Jesus knew Peter would fail. What's so beautiful, and should encourage us, is that when Peter did fail, Je-

> *God doesn't see failure when he looks at us. He sees our hearts and both what we are as well as what we are becoming.*

sus didn't fire him as a disciple or berate him and recount all his mistakes. Other people may respond that way, but not Jesus.

Instead, Jesus prayed for Peter, and he showed confidence in Peter. He let Peter know that he, God's Son, knew Peter's weaknesses and loved him anyway. And get this: Jesus even said, "Peter, I have prayed for you that your faith may not fail."[4]

Did you catch that? God is always rooting for us. He's not against us, waiting for us to mess up so he can scold us. No, he's for us. He believes in us. Jesus even prays for us.[5]

No, failure is not a person, and God's love for Peter proves it. Not long after Jesus said he was praying for Peter, our fisherman friend denied that he even knew Jesus. He made this mistake not once, but three times. In. A. Row.

Have you ever done anything that you so deeply regretted, like Peter? I have. My guess is everyone has...or will. But the beautiful thing we can learn from Peter, the thing I love, is that he didn't give up on himself—he admitted his failure. Because of that, he was able to go forward, knowing that God didn't see him as a failure but as a learner. Because, as Peter shows us, failure is not who we are. It's merely an event (or two or three) in our lives.

God understands us, especially in failure

One day, years ago when I was working in the office at the church, a man on our staff brought in his teenage son to see my dad. This father was so mad at his son for something the young man had done wrong. The father expected my dad to straighten out the son in no uncertain terms.

My dad listened to the father's grievance and boy's actions, then asked the son to step outside a moment while he spoke to his father.

My dad turned to the boy's father and gently smiled. "Don't be so hard on your son," he said. "He's a teenager. Why don't you just show him mercy? Why don't you give him another chance?"

That teenager never forgot what my dad did. Neither have I. My dad showed mercy because he had a great example: God is a God of mercy.

We forget that too much of the time. But the truth is, God is near to us and he knows how we feel. He isn't judgmental. He is understanding and compassionate, slow to anger, and rich in love.[6]

God never loses confidence in us

How many people have we lost confidence in because they disappointed us? We judge a person based on one event in his or her life, without giving a second chance.

I'm so glad that God never gives up on us, that he doesn't lose confidence in us. Though we may lose confidence in ourselves, God believes in us.

Do you believe in God's promise as much as he believes in you? What would happen if you did?

Peter offers us a great example in answer to this question. He could have remained in misery and defeat because of his failures, but he didn't. He knew that Jesus believed in him and he did, indeed, become that strong rock, as Jesus said he would. Peter became a prominent leader and an ambassador of God's great love. We are even encouraged today by his teachings in the Bible. Though Peter made some serious mistakes, even though he failed, he did not allow his failures to keep him from his destiny.

What if you had that kind of confidence in the aftermath of your own failures?

I want to say to you today that God believes in you!

I believe in you—you are made for more than being stuck in failure. You are made for success. You, too, can go from failure and disappointment into your destiny.

Don't Let a Moment Become a Lifetime

The natural question, of course, is how? After a mistake, how do you continue on toward good things?

What should we do when we fail?

1. Be honest and admit it

I've heard it said that strong people make as many mistakes as weak people. The difference is that strong people admit their mistakes and learn from them. That is how they become strong. You can try to hide behind a façade of perfection, but you will never live up to it.

Adam and Eve tried to hide their wrongdoing from God because they were embarrassed and ashamed.[7] Isn't that funny? No one can hide from God—he is all-knowing and all-seeing.

Even though Adam and Eve tried to hide, God still pursued them because he loved them in spite of their failure. There were consequences to their failure, but those consequences didn't change the way God felt about them.

TO HELP YOU MORE

True Repentance

Peter may have failed Jesus many times, but he also showed true, genuine repentance. When our children aggravate each other, I will say to them, "You need to apologize to your brother or sister."

And many times they laughingly say, "I'm sorry."

Knowing their lack of sincerity, I add, "No, say it again and act like you are sorry!"

They quickly wipe the smile off of their face and humbly say, "I'm sorry, sister or brother!" In the same way we must humble ourselves before God. We can't just pass it off lightly, and that's what we learn from Peter.

Peter sinned big time when he denied Jesus. Jesus even predicted that he would fail, but Peter argued with him and said, "Jesus, I will never deny you!"

Sometimes we mean to do right, but we fall anyway. How we respond to sin is what makes all the difference in the world. Proverbs 28:13 says that the person who conceals sin does not prosper, but whoever confesses and renounces sin finds mercy.

Peter wept bitterly over his sin, showing true sorrow and repentance. The Bible says if we confess our sins, God, who is faithful and just, will forgive us and purify us (1 John 1:9). True repentance brings about forgiveness and restoration—and it shows us that God can use us to do great things for him, even though we mess up at times.

Did you know that Jesus was thinking about Peter and was concerned for him after he sinned? After Jesus's resurrection, an angel spoke with the women who were looking for him at the empty tomb. This angel said, "Jesus is not here. He is risen." And then he said, "Go tell this good news to his disciples…and to Peter."

I love that. God wanted Peter to know that he had been forgiven and restored. Don't you know that Peter was glad to hear those words?

I want to encourage you to humble yourself before the Lord and repent of your sin. To repent means to turn around and make a change. If you are having a hard time overcoming a particular sin, don't hide it or you'll never get victory. Admit it to the Lord and ask him to help you.

When Kevin and I were first married, we had an argument because he said something that hurt my feelings. His comment wasn't serious and probably unintentional, but it bothered me. Kevin, however, couldn't see the error of his ways. In fact, he didn't think he was wrong at all.

I was mad at him, and on my way to an event, so I left the house angry. I never like to do that, but the way I saw things this was all his fault.

When I came home, Kevin met me at the door wearing a white T-shirt on which he'd written in really big letters: I WAS WRONG! I AM SORRY!

I loved it. His gesture melted me. I was so happy that he admitted it. I was more than willing to forgive and forget after that. I didn't even care about what we were arguing about anymore. I just wanted to kiss and make up.

That is how God must feel when you just say, "God, I blew it. I know I was wrong! I am sorry and I don't want to do it again." God has mercy on us when we come to him like that. He restores us to him.

Some people think God is mad at them when they sin, but that idea couldn't be further from the truth. The fact is God loves you and is pursuing you. Sin hurts us more than anything. God knows what is best for us and his desire is to instruct us in the best path for our lives.

As our family's friend Israel Houghton says, "God is not mad at you. He is madly in love with you!"

2. Separate the action from your identity

We must not allow failure, an event, to define who we are. You may have failed, but you are not a failure.

When I went through an unwanted divorce years ago, I had to work hard to wash both that divorce and that failure mentality out of my mind. At first, I saw myself as A Divorced Person, meaning someone who failed at marriage and would forever be labeled as such. But I had to change the way I saw myself. I had to realize that God always gives me a new beginning. He is able to take a negative circumstance and turn it around for our good.

Today I don't see myself as a victim or simply a label: DIVORCED. No, because of God's love and tender mercy, I see myself by this label: AN OVERCOMER.

You can do the same, no matter what your own failure. You can choose to not allow an event to define who you are or keep you from the bright future God has mapped out for you.

3. Change your focus

Most important, spend your energy on doing the things that please God. If you continually focus on your failure, you relive it over and over again.

Don't let a moment become a lifetime.

Too many of us let our lives be claimed by a failure. What a waste. Instead of focusing on our weaknesses, we need to focus on our strengths. We need to focus on our goals: to grow, to be a good mother or father or husband and wife, or person and friend, to work with excellence, and to do the things that please God. That kind of focus will override failure and get us to the great things God has in store for us.

Meet Failure with Faith

How then do we respond to failure? When our friends, coworkers, and loved ones fail, do we go over all their mistakes? Do we concentrate on what went wrong?

What if we thought first of the person, not their mistakes? People, after all, are the most important thing to God. Our Heavenly Father always reaches out to the wounded with love and mercy so that they can rise above any fall. Think what that means to you when you make a mistake—to be believed in again.

Just like the man I met on the beach, too many of us suffer alone because we are ashamed of our failure. And too often, when we're on the other side, witnessing someone's failure, we do not reach out to the fallen because we don't know what to do.

Reach out with mercy, not judgment

God always reaches out to the wounded with love and mercy so that they can rise above any fall.

I've seen the effects of this. I have a friend who went through a very public and devastating divorce a few years ago. Many people were criticizing and judging her. Even though I didn't know her well, I wanted to encourage her. I knew how painful divorce could be without public hurt added to the private grief. I e-mailed her an encouraging and hopeful message. I let her know I was praying for her.

She e-mailed me back immediately and thanked me for my support. It meant the world to her, she said.

Eventually we became friends, and later she told me that I was only one of two people who reached out to her during that tragedy.

How sad. Why is it so easy to judge others, to throw rocks at people who suddenly find themselves in glass houses by the failures that become talked about and public? The Bible says we will know people by their fruit or by their actions.[8] I once read something that elaborated on this idea: "You will know others by their fruit, but by their roots you will seek to understand them and not judge them." We don't know what they have gone through or what problems they have faced, or how we would have acted if we were faced with the same situation.

Sometimes we respond with a religious or self-righteous attitude. We treat people who have not lived up to our expectations as if they are second-class citizens. I think it is good to ask ourselves this question, "What if that were my daughter, my son?" Or, "What if that were me?" In twenty-five-plus years of working with people, I've learned that judging and condemning people never cures anybody. But, mercy triumphs over judgment, and love never fails.[9]

Be a hero to the fallen wounded

How do you practice mercy in the face of failure?

- Seek to understand people rather than judge them.
- Instead of talking about someone who has failed, talk with them.
- Rather than respond with observations on how they went wrong or things they should have done, offer them a loving attitude and a helping hand.

It is human nature to be critical and fault finding. But we are made for more than that. When I had the time to get to know my friend, I was amazed at the adversity and suffering she had endured. Failure can be so isolating. But encouragement helps free people to move forward in life.

We must train ourselves to see and believe the best in people. You have the potential to reach down and pick people up wherever you go.

Put down your rocks

You also have the potential to practice restoration. You begin when you give people the freedom to fail—because everybody fails at some point in life. If you expect perfection out of people, you will be sorely disappointed.

There is an amazing story in the Bible about a woman who was caught in the act of adultery.[10] Some religious men thought it their duty to humiliate her in public and stone her to death. (I still wonder why they didn't bring the man. I mean, what's up with that?!) They threw her at the feet of Jesus to see what he would do.

What Jesus surprised them with so reveals the heart of God. He turned to the angry crowd of accusers, then began writing in the dirt with his finger as he said: "He who is without sin is free to cast the first stone."

Huh? each man must have thought. They put down their rocks and walked away, from the oldest to the youngest.

We don't know what Jesus wrote in the sand that day, but what if it was words of failures each of these men had committed? What if Jesus scratched in the sand: LIAR. THIEF. SLANDERER. GOSSIP. CHEAT. We don't know, but what we do know is what Jesus did next. He lifted up the woman. He looked around at the men walking off. "Who are those who accuse you?" he asked the woman.

"No one, sir," she replied.

"Neither do I accuse you," he answered. "Go home and sin no more."

It's time for us to put our rocks down and seek to lift those who are fallen. Every person deserves another chance. That's why it is so important for you and me to seek to restore people and not just write them off. The Bible says, "Do to others what you would want them to do for you."[11] We call this the Golden Rule, but these are divinely inspired words from our loving Heavenly Father.

Think of the restoration, not the retribution

That is what God wants, after all: to love us, to restore us to his love. He wants us to practice such love and restoration like he does.

Bringing restoration to others can be as simple as:

- sending a note to encourage.
- calling to show you care.
- being there to listen.
- loving no matter what, without condition.

Every person needs encouragement. What you make happen for others will happen for you. When you reach out to restore those who have fallen, you are sowing seeds for your own future and setting yourself up to win. Show kindness to those who are hurting, and you will find love, restoration, and kindness in your future. As you reach down to lift others up out of failure, you will be empowered to rise up over every failure and adversity into the wonderful plans God has prepared for you.

It's Your Day to Get Back Up

I heard someone say once, "I'm either up or getting back up."[12] That's the attitude we should have. Don't even entertain the thought of allowing failure to defeat you and keep you down.

What a great definition of true failure, because we all experience failure. We misstep, fall, fail. But choosing not to get up again? That is the real failure.

The Bible says that though we may fall even seven times, we should rise again.[13] God is saying to us: *I don't look for your failures. I look for your heart and your progress.*

Isn't that encouraging? God's not keeping score of our every mistake, like an Olympic judge. God's more like the coach at the finish line beckoning us to cross with flying colors. He's rooting for us. He wants us up and running toward bigger and better things, showing even ourselves to be the winners he made us to be.

We're all in training. Each of us is a work in progress. Maybe we should have signs on our foreheads that say, CONSTRUCTION ZONE, for the Bible declares we are God's workmanship, and he is not finished with us yet.[14] Every day, whether we realize it or not, we are growing and making progress in our lives. You will see that the weaknesses you have today will soon be a thing of the past, if you refuse to allow failure to stop you.

Of course that may be the trickiest thing about failure: forgiving ourselves for the mistakes we make. Often, we are so much harder on ourselves than anyone else can be. But when we fail, we must choose to forgive ourselves.

If our children came to Kevin and me to ask forgiveness because of something they had done wrong, how sad it would be if, after getting that forgiveness, they hang their heads in hopelessness and say, "We just can't forgive ourselves. We will never get over this. We are failures!"

That would break our hearts!

So it is with our Heavenly Father. When we hang on to our own failure (or someone else's), his heart breaks. He longs for us to release our failures and hold up our heads high with confidence. He wants us to begin again. He wants us to know, like I wanted that man by the beach to know, that we are not washed up by failure.

Our mistakes cause us to fall, yes. Like a stone sinking to the bottom of the ocean, failure can weigh us down. But God will bring waves of mercy that toss us back upon a new shore. God has a great plan in mind, just as Jesus had for Peter, the rock—because it's a funny thing about those waves and all that tossing: it smoothes all your rough edges. It humbles you. It makes you beautiful and you realize how strong you are, and you find yourself on a new shore, ready for something new that God has in store, ready to pick someone else up when they fall.

11

Finding More When You Feel Unable

*Because You're Fully Equipped
to Do and Be More*

∽

I'm blessed to drive a wonderful car, my dad's twelve-year-old Lexus. After he died in 1999, the family decided I should use his car, and it has been a gift. I drove the car for eight years, though, before I discovered by accident two features that I never knew existed! I learned I could use the key remote to roll down the windows, and that there was a button to adjust the headrests. Can you believe it? I had been adjusting the headrests manually, and it's a wonder that I hadn't broken them because they didn't adjust without a struggle. If I had just read the manual, I could have enjoyed these features all those years.

That is just like what happens with us. We sometimes miss that God has completely equipped us for our purpose in life. He has fully empowered us for our destiny. But we forget to read our manual, the Bible. We miss that he has wired us for more than we realized. We get stuck believing that we lack something. Or we think we're limited and unable because others don't approve of us or appreciate us.

God says: *No. I made you for more so that you can run your race. You're not unable. I made you complete for what you need to do and be. I made you the best for your unique destiny. You're my top-of-the-line model.*[1]

We're each a Lexus, but why do we believe we are lemons? Today I want you to begin to see yourself fully equipped and able to fulfill your destiny.

You are what I like to call a Triple A person:

Appointed.

Anointed.

And Approved.

God has already appointed you, anointed you, and approved you to do great things, to make a difference in your world. How much the world and God—and our very selves!—miss, though, when we fail to fuel up on his promises of this.

Knowing What You're Made Of

Tracey missed so much for a good deal of her life. She never saw her abilities and greatness, her Lexus appeal. She grew up in a Christian home with what she describes as a charmed childhood, even making a commitment at eight years old to follow Christ. Then crisis hit her family.

A life-altering car accident left one of her two brothers a paraplegic. Then, seven days before her fifteenth birthday, her father died after a heart attack. Her mother lost her partner, protector, and provider. Tracey's brothers lost a best friend, their role model. Tracey said that was the beginning of her losing herself. She didn't know how to grieve or mourn. Not having received therapeutic care or counseling, she wrestled throughout her high school and college years with a profound sense of loss and pain.

"The fifteen years that followed my father's death became simply about pain management," she says. "Alcohol, drugs, and sex became commonplace. Other self-hate coping behaviors followed: adrenaline junkie, control freak, fear of germs, body dimorphic, agoraphobic, workaholic, perfectionist. All these behaviors had a respective hold on my life at some point. I felt so utterly devastated that I even denied my natural inclinations and created a new personality for myself."

Quiet by nature, precocious and creative, Tracey began to exhibit extreme anger and aggression. She became loud, obnoxious, audacious, and brazen. "I masked any of my true abilities, talents, gifts, and interests," she says. "My self-identity eventually became the colors of the chameleon. With every new change,

I believed things would be better for me, and then it would be the next change that would fix me, and then the next thing would make me better."

In the confusion of trying to be someone, anyone, but her wounded self, Tracey lost the will to live. But something in her remembered the God of her youth.

"I started begging a very faraway, historic, and irrelevant God to let me die," she says. "I resigned myself to the thought that death would be better than the emotional pain and chaos that I had become accustomed to living with on a daily basis."

Desperate, she found her way to Lakewood. It took false courage to get there, she says: "I hate to admit that I was chemically altered those first few visits." But she longed for release. She wanted to give God another try.

"Even in that altered state," she says, "I heard from God. That very first visit, I heard God say, *I see you.*"

Tracey wondered: *Is what I'm hearing for real?* Curiosity drew her back to church again. And again. Within a month she wanted to see if she could hear from God when she wasn't altered by drugs in her system. "I had to know if that voice was for real and not my imagination or hallucinations."

The voice was real. *I love you,* she heard. *I am so proud of you.* God told Tracey he made her for more, and that he had designed and equipped her for a life of victory and freedom.

"Those were words I had been craving for fifteen years," Tracey says. "God melted me down to my very core that day and has every day since."

Tracey began to actively pursue the God who saw her, made her, and knew her better than she knew herself. She began to work on releasing her addictions and coping mechanisms, and rest in the freedom of a God who empowered her. "Experiencing a true, personal relationship with God became a better high," she says, "than any other."

One day Tracey was asked to imagine what her life would be like after another year, and, even further, five years down the road. She hoped and dreamed she would be able to help others, to live a good life herself, to be a person who made God proud.

Five years later, Tracey says she's not churchy, just loved, empowered, and equipped to do and be more. "I could say that I don't recognize my life, but that would be a mistruth," she explains. "I am more like the little girl I was before the loss of my earthly father. God has restored me to the precociousness, creativity, and calm that I had as a child. The walls of the façade that I had built have crumbled brick by brick over the years, exposing the beauty, truth, love, freedom, and hope that had been buried in what seems like an entire lifetime ago. I find it interesting that he is using the experiences of my fifteen-year detour into hopelessness and confusion to help those around me.

I look forward to each day and its divine appointments. There is still more to learn, more to yearn for, more to experience, and that is my prayer to him: *More God, more, please.* He continues to work on me, meeting me right where I am, just as he has always done. And when it gets difficult, I simply ask for encouragement. To which he promptly replies, *I see you, little girl, and I love you so much.*"

Just as she felt more lost than the lost, Tracey says, she was found.

The God Who Sees

That is what God waits for all of us to find: That we are never lost to him, that he sees us and knows us, and made us Triple A people. That means he made you a Lexus in a lemon world. He equips you with everything you need to overcome obstacles and adversity, and fulfill your destiny. He sees you as a vital part of his plan, and there are people out there who need what only you have to offer.

The Bible says: "We are assured and know that…all things work together and are [fitting into a plan] for good—to and for those who love God and are called according to [his] design and purpose."[2] God is saying: *You are called and designed for my purposes. You are handcrafted specifically for your destiny, a mission ordained by me that only you can fulfill.*

He doesn't just give you a purpose and send you into the unknown to complete it. No, he loads you with what you need, when you rely upon him, to accomplish your destiny. He's proud of you and he loves just how he made you, even the parts that you don't love yourself.

Your shyness, for example, just might be his design that gives you the heart to get others who are shy to open up and share. Your tendency to put up a fight might be his construct so you can endure great attacks in a public office and never give up or give in. Your hypersensitivity may be his plan for your perceptiveness as an artist.

Sometimes you don't realize what you're made of, and you don't see how complete God designed you. Other times there are people who call out things about you to make you think you're unable, incapable, or unqualified for the very things God designed you to do.

Sometimes you don't know what you're made of, and you don't see how complete God designed you.

A perfect picture of this is in the film *The Sound of Music*. Remember the scene where all the other nuns are complaining about Maria? She's late. She daydreams. She runs off to the hills and mountains and gets lost in nature. She sings in the garden without permission, and even in the abbey when it is not time to sing. But singing and dreaming and passionately filling the day with every possible adventure are what make Maria wonderful. They are what attract the Captain to her, and enable her to reunite the relationships in his family—and endure all the cruel days of flight across the Alps from the Nazis. The very things her fellow nuns had complained about in song at the beginning of the film are the things they sing about to Maria's glory on her wedding day. They are the very things that enable Maria to help her new family reach their destiny.

I've gone through seasons when I was convinced that I wasn't equipped to do anything for God. I thought I didn't possess this or that necessary feature. So many people in the Bible were like this, too. Moses didn't think he could speak eloquently.[3] Zaccheus thought he was too short to be seen by Jesus, let alone entertain him one day.[4]

But God does not make mistakes. He has done a wonderful work in each of us.[5] He makes everything perfect for its time, and sometimes the issue is not what we lack, but that we don't feel qualified or confident. God says to you: *You are qualified because I equipped you. You are not alone because I have given you my Holy Spirit to live and dwell in you.*

Jesus tells us that the Holy Spirit is your:

- helper,[6]
- counselor,[7]
- teacher,[8]
- advocate,[9]
- strengthener,[10]
- intercessor,[11]
- comforter,[12] and
- standby, ever ready to help you.[13]

Wow! The Holy Spirit, who dwells in you, is actually standing by to help you on your journey in this life. Do you see how completely God has equipped you to overcome any obstacle and to run your race? Believe that you are a Triple A person:

You are appointed.

You are anointed.

You are approved.

You Are Appointed to Fulfill Your Destiny

You have been handpicked by God, chosen by him for specific tasks: *You did not choose me, but I chose you and appointed you to go and bear much fruit.*[14] We are God's ambassadors, and he has assignments for each of us to fulfill.[15]

Whatever that appointment is, take joy in it. Maybe you are appointed to be a mom, so you spend most of your days cooking and feeding, cleaning and caring. Then your two-year-old has a tantrum and you feel yourself losing it. But grace washes over you and equips you to handle the little storm and you know: *I can do this!* And there is joy.

Or maybe you are a businessman who is tired of working with unpleasant people—and not only that, you are stressed out by your busy schedule. Just when you think, *I can't take this anymore,* God whispers in your ear: *You can. You're making a difference. Be faithful because you are representing me.*

Whatever you are appointed to do is important because you have been chosen and appointed by God to be his representative in the earth.

The Bible says, *And whatever you do or say, do it as a representative of the Lord Jesus, giving thanks through him to God the Father.*[16] That means you are his hands and feet, doing his work at home and at work, or wherever you go. So do it with all your heart. Be the best you can be at it. God promises to use you, with all your strengths and weaknesses, in what he has purposed.[17]

We, as individuals, can change our world for the

better if we are willing to accomplish the assignments that God has for us.

Sam Martin, my father's high school classmate, knew this. Sam loved God and spreading God's love everywhere he went. He would get to class early and write encouraging Scriptures on the chalkboard. Many times he talked to my dad about knowing God in a personal way, but Daddy was a little embarrassed of Sam, avoiding him when possible. Sam's persistence, however, got to my father.

One night, at the age of seventeen, Daddy was coming home from a nightclub in Fort Worth, Texas, when he began to think about eternity. He knew something was missing in his life, a void that nothing or no one could fill. That night, he called Sam and asked him to meet him at church the next morning. My dad beat Sam to the church, and after the service Daddy met the pastor and gave his life to serve God.

My dad's life was changed forever and set on a new course that morning. He had dropped out of school, but he went back and his grades improved tremendously. Like Sam, he began to tell everyone about his newfound life and freedom. Daddy started preaching wherever he was welcomed that year and eventually went to college and seminary. Until Daddy passed away in 1999, he preached the Gospel to thousands of people every week at Lakewood and millions more through the *John Osteen* television program.

All because Sam recognized he was appointed by God to be an ambassador for him. Just think how Sam changed my father's life, and my life, and eventually millions of lives around the world. One person—you—can influence your world and generations to come when you recognize that you are chosen and appointed by God to represent him on this earth.

TO HELP YOU MORE

Taking on God's Assignment: An Example

Whatever God has called you to do, you can do it with excellence, joy, and a heart of gratitude recognizing that every person has a different assignment.

My friend, Debra, is passionate about leading people to Christ. We are all called to lead people to Jesus, but I think Debra has a special assignment from God in this area. She and I could be out somewhere together having lunch, and the next thing I know she is leading our waiter to the Lord.

One time, she was on her way home and saw a group of teenagers playing basketball. She felt impressed to share the Gospel with them. She didn't know any of them, but she knew that was her assignment.

So she went over and said, "Guys, I am your neighbor and I need to tell you something."

She ended up leading every one of those teens to the Lord. Then, amazingly, a few of their mothers came out and asked to pray the Salvation Prayer with them.

My friend was just being obedient in her assignment—and God used her in a powerful way. He'll use you, too, if you will just step out and obey him in your assignment.

God promises: if you will be faithful to him in the little things, he will trust you with more (Luke 14:12–14). And it all begins by knowing that God chose you and appointed you to fulfill your destiny.

Your assignment may change

Know this, however: once you find your appointment, your assignment can still change. That's why we must be willing to listen for God and move on to the next assignment. That's a part of fulfilling your destiny.

For seventeen years, I served my mother and father at Lakewood Church. While my brother, Joel, was working in the television department, I was the director of ministries. That was my assignment, and I gave it my very best.

In 1999, my assignment changed. Our beloved daddy died and went to be with the Lord. Not only was that event so hard for me because I lost my daddy, but I also lost my boss, my mentor, and my pastor. For the first week after his death, I thought, *What am I going to do now?* As a church, we were venturing into the unknown. *Who will be the pastor? What will my position be? Will people continue to attend church?* It was all so different now.

The next Sunday, Joel stepped up and decided to preach. We were ecstatic. Before Joel walked onto the platform, he was sitting in the front row where our daddy always sat. I was sitting behind him and leaned up to tell him something, just like I had done many times with our father.

In that instant, God impressed upon me: *Just as you served your father, I am transitioning you now to serve your brother.*

The words were so real, God's plan so real, that I felt this surge of joy. I suddenly saw how God had something more in store all along. My assignment wasn't over. It had just changed. In the way that I had supported my father, I could now support my brother. In the days ahead, I began to speak at the Wednesday services on a regular basis and help in new areas.

When I had been concerned about the changes, God had something greater ahead for me. That's why we must be flexible and willing to make changes as God directs us.

You Are Anointed

It's a mysterious word, *anointing*. But an anointing, simply put, is God's power at work in and through you. The best description I can give of the anointing is this: God's grace, strength, ability, and power to do what he has called you to do. His anointing empowers you to be all that he's called you to be. Not only does his anointing empower you to use your gifts, but it empowers you to get through any trial you may face.

This anointing abides permanently in us. It is not something that comes upon us once in a while. You do not have to pray and ask for the anointing. You do not have to work for it or earn it. You are anointed because you belong to God and his Spirit dwells in you. You are the temple of God's Holy Spirit.[18] As the Bible says: "The anointing you received abides permanently in you—it remains in you."[19]

Think about that for a moment. The Bible is saying you are a container of God's power. His grace, power, strength, and ability are always available to you.

When you think of it that way, it's easier to understand how you are anointed and supernaturally empowered for your everyday life. God puts his super on your natural so that you can accomplish the very things he has called you to do.

Being anointed means God enables you when you don't feel able

Does that mean there are times we won't feel able to do what God has in store? Of course! We are human. Each of us will have times when we don't feel anointed to do what God has called us to do, but that's when we must trust God's Word beyond our feelings.

I will never forget the first time my father asked me to preach for him while he was away traveling. This was in 1985. Our church had about four thousand people, and this would be the first time I stood in my dad's place. He had big shoes to fill. I felt like people were expecting a lot and that they were curious, too, wondering, *Is she any good at speaking? Can a girl do what her dad is a pro at doing?* I was so nervous.

So I prepared and studied. I knew I wanted to speak on the armor of God and how we are equipped for every trial in life, whatever we face.[20]

That Sunday, even though I had prepared and studied my heart out, that first minute and a half behind the pulpit, I didn't feel so equipped at all. I struggled. My legs were shaking and my voice was quivering as I clung closely to the pulpit and my notes. In a moment of desperation, I took a slight step back from the pulpit and in my heart said, *God, I need your help!*

What happened to me next is hard to describe. For years I didn't share this story with anyone because it is so personal. But now I realize that what God did for me is a picture of what he does for each of his children.

When I stepped back from the pulpit, all of a sudden it was as if I was out of my body looking down and watching myself preach. I saw myself struggling for the right words to say, and then I saw and felt something almost invisible, yet tangible, come down from above and onto me. I know it sounds strange, but at that moment I knew that God was allowing me to see that he had anointed me and equipped me for the job to which he had called me. I felt a powerful sense, like God reached down and wrapped me in his grace and a huge mantle.

When I stepped back up to the pulpit, I sensed a definite difference. I had a boldness and confidence that I didn't have before. I felt more secure, more sure: *I can do this.* I knew God was with me! I understood that I was anointed.

You, too, are anointed.

Jesus said the Holy Spirit is our helper, and we can

trust him to empower us in our time of need. Jesus knew this as a man. When he walked the earth, he relied on the power of the Holy Spirit to help him fulfill his mission.[21] That's how God wants us to live—fully dependent on the Holy Spirit in every area of our lives. The Holy Spirit will guide us, teach us, lead us, pray through us, and empower us.

Jesus even tells us why he was anointed and why we are anointed: "The Spirit of the Lord is upon me, for he has anointed me to bring Good News to the poor. He has sent me to proclaim that captives will be released, that the blind will see, that the oppressed will be set free, and that the time of the Lord's favor has come."[22]

You may be thinking, *Yes, but that is Jesus.* But in his own words Jesus told us: *Anyone who believes in me will do the works that I did.*

Isn't that wonderful? Jesus was anointed to help people, and he's saying, *So are you.* God has empowered you so he can use you to set people free. You may not be in the full-time ministry, but you are anointed to help people everywhere you go.

Not long ago, I was in the shopping mall when a man stopped me and introduced himself as a member of Lakewood Church. He began to tell me about some difficult things he was going through.

"Let me pray for you," I offered, and reached for his hands.

The man said, "Are you going to do it right now?"

I said, "Yes, if you don't mind." He agreed and left encouraged.

I didn't want to miss an opportunity to help right when help was needed. I know how prayer changes things—and I believe I am anointed to help people.

TO HELP YOU MORE

You Can Be Someone's Divine Appointment Today

When you begin to realize you're a Triple A person—appointed, anointed, and approved —you begin to see how God arranges divine appointments everywhere. I'm talking about those meetings and interactions that some people might call a coincidence but you know are from God.

An example is a couple years ago, when my mother and I headed to the airport. Traffic was heavy, and the clock moved ahead but we didn't. We were doing what we knew to do as Triple A people, heading to speak at a conference hosted by dear friends. But time seemed against us. Even when we finally got to the airport, all the parking lots were full to capacity. We circled round and round, and when we finally found a spot we knew we were seriously in danger of missing our flight.

It didn't help that at the security check, there was a long line.

As we began to fret, a friendly gentleman recognized my mother. "How are you?" he asked, to which Mother admitted, "I'm concerned we're going to miss our flight."

Without missing a beat, this kind man grabbed my mother's hand and said, "Follow me!" He took us through security in a flash, and escorted us to our gate. But he was big, strong, and athletic, and quickly way ahead of us. We struggled to keep up—and he noticed. He spotted an empty wheelchair and said to mother, "Ms. Dodie, get in and I will take you to your gate."

Mother politely declined, but this fellow wouldn't take no for an answer.

"Go ahead," I told mother. "I'll be right behind you."

Off this fellow went, pushing Mother in the wheelchair as then I struggled to keep up. As I began to fall behind once again (I told you this guy was fast!), our escort noticed. He spotted another wheelchair and said, "Lisa, jump in!"

My pride put on its brakes. There was no way I was going to get in that wheelchair. "It's okay," I said. "I'll meet up with you."

But our friend wouldn't take no for an answer. He practically scooped me into the wheelchair, saying, "If you don't let me help you, then you're going to miss your plane."

He was right, so I settled into the chair and he took off, one hand on each wheelchair, pushing us down the terminal. He was amazing, strong, and fast!

And I was embarrassed, ashamed to have someone have to push me in a wheelchair when I could walk. I groped for my sunglasses to at least go undercover a bit.

"What in the world are you doing?" Mother asked.

"Put your sunglasses on and look down," I answered. "Don't let anybody see who we are, like we're getting special treatment!"

Without another question she agreed, as our benefactor kept pushing us along, paying no attention to our efforts to be invisible. He was on a mission and he refused to be distracted. He was a divine appointment for us, helping us get to our gate just in the nick of time to catch our flight.

He might not have seen himself that way that day, but this kind man helped Mother and I keep our divine appointment at that conference. You can be someone's divine appointment today, too, and as you are faithful to help others, God will always have your divine appointments waiting for you.

Being anointed means you can serve God right here, right now

That's what being anointed means: You have a calling to act right when and where you're needed. When you're called, you're called wherever you are!

A similar incident happened a couple of years ago when I went to get my nails done. My manicurist greeted me warmly and asked if I would put her sister on our prayer list at Lakewood. Her sister, a mother of young children, had just learned she had an aggressive cancer. Her prognosis was not positive, and she was scheduled for surgery immediately. Of course, she and her family were devastated. I told this lady that I would definitely put her sister on our prayer list.

But as she was finishing my nails I didn't feel like I had completed my assignment. After all, this was a divine appointment, and this woman was visibly upset about her sister. I didn't know how she would respond, but I said quietly, "Can we pray right now?" She agreed and I moved close to her ear and prayed, asking God to heal her sister, to cause the surgery to be a success so that she could raise her family and fulfill her destiny.

When I finished, the woman looked at me and said, "I've never experienced anything like that. I've never heard anyone before pray like that."

It was the anointing of the Holy Spirit that touched her heart. God will fuel you, just like a Lexus is run on gasoline, to step up and do well in your appointment and assignment.

Interestingly, two months later, when I went back to the manicurist, she told me her sister had gone in for surgery as scheduled, but something incredible happened. The doctors were stunned as they viewed new X-rays and compared them to the previous ones. There were no signs of cancer in the new X-rays. The family was ecstatic. They took the miracle as a direct answer to their prayers.

"Lisa," the manicurist said, "I want you to tell every person what God did for my sister!"

God's power will work through you when you recognize you are anointed to help and encourage people wherever you go.

You are approved to fulfill your destiny

At the end of my first year of college, I decided to apply for a position in our dorm as a chaplain. This would mean overseeing a group of about thirty girls, encouraging them, praying with them, and conducting devotions. My brother Paul was a chaplain's director at the time, and I always loved hearing about the richness of his experience.

So I filled out the application for the job and went through the interview. Then I waited.

The news came: I was not approved to be chosen as a chaplain. The team hiring didn't think I was ready, and, they added, I seemed too shy.

Too shy? I sighed inside. I knew that was true. I *was* shy. Maybe I wasn't ready, and yet, and yet...I felt a desire to help people. In any case, I decided to just let go of my idea that I could do this, and I went home for the summer break.

Two weeks before the fall semester was to begin, I got a surprise call from the Chaplain's Department. Did I still want to be a chaplain in the dorm? Could I start with the fall term that was about to begin?

At first I couldn't believe my ears. *Was I hearing right?* Then, it was explained, one of the approved chaplains could not return to school. She dropped out, and her position as a dorm chaplain was vacated. The department needed someone to take her place.

I was so happy! I was second choice, but I got the job, even if it was by default.

As I learned in college, people will not always approve you. They may not always be able to see the potential in you. But God does, and his approval will make way for his plan.

Do you believe that for your life? You are accepted by God and approved by him for all eternity. That means you have God's stamp of approval upon your life. The Bible says that God has "anointed us, set his seal of ownership on us, and put his Spirit in our hearts as a deposit, guaranteeing what is to come."[23] Jesus's disciples said, "We speak as men approved by God to be entrusted with the Gospel."[24]

God's got his stamp on you

Have you ever thought about the meaning of a postmark on the letters you receive in the mail? That little circle stamped over the postage verifies the date and place where the letter was mailed from. The symbol is verification that the letter is authentic and its cost to deliver has been paid, that it indeed has a destiny and has been sent to that destiny by an authority, the US Postal Service.

So it is with you and me. We are postmarked,

sealed, and stamped by God. His mark shows three things: his authority, authentification, and destiny. He stamps us with his authority for our destinies, which he created and designed. When God thinks about us and looks at us he says: *I approve!*

Would you try to argue with him, saying, "But God, I'm not qualified. What about my past? I don't think I can do that."

The past doesn't matter, God says. Stamp! *You're already approved! And your fear? My Spirit will help you with that. And your inability? Where you are weak, I am strong.*[25]

I remember seeing a funny commercial many years ago that I have never forgotten. This man was obsessed with his new label maker and was caught in the act. Not only had he labeled his files, but he had labels all over his body. So when I think of how God has accepted and approved of me, I see in my imagination his stamp of approval all over me! There's nothing about me that he rejects. He accepts me, faults and all.[26] He desires to use me whether I'm qualified or not. He has chosen to appoint me, anoint me, and approve of me.

Think about that. God Almighty, the creator of the universe, the only perfect one, approves of you today. That means that you have his unconditional acceptance, love, and blessing. It doesn't matter where you've come from, it doesn't matter what you've done, it doesn't matter what anybody else has said about you. You are approved by Almighty God.

His approval frees you from comparisons and conforming

When you understand that you are approved by God, it will set you free from trying to compare yourself with others.

Yes, it's good to receive encouragement from others, but when God tells you to do something, you don't need to wear yourself out trying to please people. You don't need to be devastated if you don't get their approval. When God has a plan, he will make it happen in the right time, in the right way. Isn't that freeing? You don't have to figure it all out. He's already done that!

Did you know that also means God will never anoint you to become someone else?

He tells us: *Don't dare compare yourself to others.*[27] God has anointed you to be you. You don't need to look at the strengths of other people and, instead of appreciating them, put down yourself. Cheer on others and celebrate them. But you also need to celebrate yourself. You're approved by God, too. Be confident in who God made you to be.

If you look at my mother and all of my sisters and brothers, we are alike in many ways. And yet each of us has our own unique style of speaking and ministry. We are each different. I love the way God did that. Celebrate the way God made you by being yourself. He likes the way he made you, and you are designed for your own destiny. God didn't call us to be copy-cats. He called us to be originals.

Your Triple A Status Began in Your Beginning

As a young girl, I hadn't dreamed of becoming a Bible teacher and preacher, a minister. But those stirrings came as I grew.

Looking back, I see how as a teenager, I had a desire not only to read the Bible but to study the Bible. My parents taught us by example how to read our Bible every day. They would rise early, and my mother would make our breakfast before school. But while we were scurrying around the house getting ready, she and my dad would be sitting in their recliners reading their Bibles and praying.

My brothers and sisters and I saw their faithfulness to listen to God and know him. We saw the peace it gave them personally, and us, and our home, and those who crossed their paths. We longed for that same peace. We each tried to follow in their footsteps. For us, then, reading our Bibles every morning was just a part of getting dressed for the day. Now I can see how God used that to place in each of us a love for him. For me, it also stirred an intense desire to study the Bible, and when I went through a dark time as a young woman, distracted by my own brokenness and feelings of unworthy disqualification, God was at work again.

He had already approved and anointed me. Now he was making clear my assignment. He got me started in small ways, first praying with others, then teaching, then preaching.

I remember, as a little girl and then a young woman, listening to my father preach. How I loved him. How he moved me with his love and relationship with God. I developed a desire to preach. And God was making the way for that, just like God has been making the way for that small stirring in you.

What is that stirring? Is it to start your own business? Is it a desire to make a difference in the political realm?

Your destiny is already in motion.

You are already Triple A ready: appointed, anointed, and approved. God has the road map for this future. He will give you the directions, and you can find his guidance in the Bible, through prayer and through listening for him in your daily life. He's equipped you to be loaded and ready, and what you cannot do he will do through you by his grace. He sees you like he saw Tracey—the real you, the wonderful you. He knows your purpose, like he knew mine before even I did. He believes in the good you can do for others. He's all about showing you that you can go the distance, like the best Lexus, because all along he's equipped you with *more.*

12
Finding More
When You're Ready to Give Up

Because You're Made to Keep On—and to
Win

∽

At eleven years old, I liked visiting a friend who lived on the next street over from ours. She had horses, and she taught me how to ride and even do a few jumping tricks.

My friend also liked to taunt her horses, and one day she encouraged me to join in the teasing. We pretended to feed her horse an apple. Before giving over the sweet fruit, though, we pulled the apple away, leaving that poor horse biting into nothing but thin air. We then ran away, trying to get the horse to chase us.

Well, the taunt worked. That horse got plain mad at us. He snorted and took off running. He ran hard.

Laughing, I looked behind. I saw that horse coming at us, nostrils flaring, and gulped. I stopped laughing and looked ahead again. *Uh-oh.* A fence. A tall one. *I cannot jump that fence,* I thought, my mind starting to race as fast as my legs. *It's too high!* Then I looked over my shoulder again. The horse was gaining ground. *How can I jump that fence?* everything in me shouted. *That horse is going to bite my rear end!*

You know, it's amazing how you can do things you don't think you can.

When I got to the fence, my adrenaline must have kicked in, because I put one foot on the bottom post and leaped over like nobody's business. You could say it was my Michael Jordan moment. I hopped that fence just like Michael leaping to slam-dunk a basketball: in a single push.

I can laugh at that now. It's funny now because I'm far from that horse and I'm not fenced in by anything high. At the time, though, I was simply relieved. I didn't think I could jump the fence...but I did.

Apparently I had more in me than I thought.

You Have More in You Than You Think

On the hard days of life, God reminds me of that incident. There have been so many times when I thought I could not make it one more day.

You know those days. You are tired and worn out. You're weary in body, mind, and spirit. You feel undone and unable. Then something kicks in and helps you, and you find yourself in tomorrow. You did make it. You can keep going. You have more in you than you thought.

That *more* is God. That *more* is his grace.

The Bible tells us God will sustain us: you can lie down and sleep at night and wake again because the Lord sustains you.[1] I have learned that when I am tempted to feel overwhelmed at the end of the day, the best thing I can do is go to bed! Because when I get up in the morning, I find that God sustains me. I did make it another day just like he promised. And I will continue to make it.

God is faithful. He promises to not allow you to be tempted and tried beyond your ability and strength and power to endure. He will help you to be strong and powerful, to bear up patiently.[2] God tells each of us: *You have more in you than you realize. You are made to win, not to be defeated.*[3] *You are made to receive my promise.*[4]

All of us go through hardships in this life. Yours may be particularly hard. Whatever you are dealing with, you've got to know that nothing is too difficult for God. You may be tired and weary, but God will bring you through this. He promises: *What you are going through is temporary and subject to change. But one thing will never change and that is my Word, my promises, which are eternal.*[5] I often turn to Psalm 23 for comfort, because in that simple shepherd's song is a great promise: though we walk through valleys—

dark, low places—the truth is that God will get us through. He doesn't want us to stop in the valley and camp there forever. He wants us to keep following him so he, as the great shepherd, can get us to mountaintops. He will direct our steps and get us to a place of hope again—and will make the hope real.

David, the shepherd who wrote the Twenty-Third Psalm, said, "I have pitched my tent in the land of hope."[6] Too often, too many of us pitch a tent in the valley, in the place of hopelessness.

But Hebrews 10:35–36 (NIV) says, "So do not throw away your confidence; it will be richly rewarded. You need to persevere so that when you have done the will of God, you will receive what he has promised."

There is strategy in that promise for facing and winning the battles of life. There is a way through the heartbreak you may have now, or the financial ruin, or the illness. There is a way to overcome the disappointment you have, or the hurt caused by your children or people you thought were friends. There is a way beyond the despair of losing people or places you loved—and it's simple to know, though sometimes challenging to practice.

Yet even in the practice of this strategy God is there with another promise. He promises to help you jump the hurdles, because he is not a God of empty promises. He longs to make good on every one, just for you, just for me. He takes joy in seeing us taste the sweetness of his promises, if we will but:

- keep our confidence in him,
- persevere in patient faithfulness, and
- do his will.

Keep Your Confidence in God

If you live long enough, you know life will try to steal your confidence in God. Things happen that you never dream. Tragedy strikes. Bombs go off. Loves are lost. Health issues arise. Dreams die.

In the midst of problems, through every trial, you are tempted to give up on your dreams, to give up on yourself, to give up on God. The hurdles to believing seem too high. The cost seems too much. You must give up control you never had. You must believe God will work all things to your benefit. You must do all this even though the timing seems bad and the way is dark or unclear, even when you think things will never change, even when you feel trapped in your situation, even when you think: *How can any good ever come to pass?*

That is because God has a plan. He is at work for you. He is for you. He wants you to hang on because he's preparing something good, and sometimes it takes some doing to bring about: some work in you and around you, some things you may never see or know.

No matter. God is still at work in you and in this world to fulfill his Word. The Bible tells us that this is the confidence that we have in him, that, if we ask anything according to his will, he hears us, and if we know that he hears us, whatever we ask, we know that we have the petitions that we desired of him.[7]

That's the kind of unshakeable confidence we can have in God.

TO HELP YOU MORE

You Can Make It with Prayer

Twenty years ago, Kevin and I accompanied my father on a trip to India, along with Joel and Victoria. We loved India, meeting the people, encouraging the leaders, and teaching the Bible. Yet this trip was the most challenging I'd faced. Going into a foreign country always takes some adjustment, but I wasn't prepared for what that meant here.

We stayed in a government house that was indeed grand compared to the impoverished sadness we saw even outside its doors: people in rags, begging for pennies. But it is one thing, when you're young, to think, *I will help these people out of their physical and spiritual misery,* and it is another to face the reality of living among their conditions.

The government house was simple, concrete, each room equipped with twin beds that had two-inch mattresses, ripped in several places. The worn carpet looked multiple times older than we did. I found myself unable to shower for five days because I felt cleaner than the bathroom and because of our constant visitors: lizards and roaches. Outside our room, lots of cute little monkeys climbed about the trees, but our host warned us to keep our distance as they were dangerous, carried disease, and could be aggressive.

Our surroundings were unsettling to me. We poured ourselves out in ministry, teaching and spending time with the people in the mornings, afternoons, and each night. Then it seemed such a low point to return to our room. For me, there was no rest. One night, we came home to several roaches crawling all over my mattress.

We weren't eating well, either, haunted by so many starving people and with so many differences in the food. We relied on canned tuna and peanut butter that we'd brought in our suitcases, and warm bottles of Coca-Cola. In one place, though, we ate fresh fish and wonderful curry at a dimly lit restaurant, and we were especially excited to see apple pie on the menu.

Joel said, "I'll order a piece and we can see if we like it." That sounded good to Victoria and me. After eating half the slice, enjoying each bite, Joel offered the other half to us. But when he pushed the plate toward Victoria and me, there was more light on our side of the table. We could see what Joel couldn't. That slice of pie was full of green, fuzzy mold.

Victoria and I cracked up laughing, incredulous and shocked that Joel had eaten half this piece of pie already.

"Well," Joel said, grinning, "I just had apple pie a la mold."

I wasn't so agreeable on our trip. The first two days all I did was complain to Kevin: "I can't believe how bad this place is. I don't think I can make it for five days." The idea of roaches and lizards crawling over me as I slept gave me chills and made me want to jump up and run outside—only there were dangerous monkeys out there. I couldn't rest.

Finally Kevin said to me, "Lisa, you might as well stop complaining because that is not going to change anything—and we are not going to leave early."

I hated to admit it, but he was right! So I decided to quit saying I couldn't make it. Instead I starting saying all day to myself, "I can do all things through Christ who strengthens me. His grace is helping me."

The night after I challenged myself with God's promises I truly slept better. Then the next night, I was sleeping like a baby. On the fifth and last night, I woke up and felt the bed swaying back and forth, but fell back to sleep.

Alarmed, Kevin woke me. "Lisa," he exclaimed, "did you feel that?"

"Yeah," I mumbled sleepily.

"I think it's an earthquake!" he said excitedly.

"I do, too," I yawned, and went right back to sleep.

Kevin spent the rest of the night awake, and in the morning we learned that the tremors we felt in the night were indeed from an earthquake two hundred miles away.

And that is the way God works. When we don't think we can make it through, he delivers strength and grace to us to get through mold, roaches, lizards, monkeys, even an earthquake.

You, too, can do more than you think. You are

> made for more. A prayer and a choice to believe
> in God's promises will get you there.

When you're in doubt, remember believers are receivers

Look at David, the young shepherd boy who faced
a giant that was killing his people, even their hope.[8]
David faced Goliath with only five small stones and
a slingshot. At least that was what people on the battlefield saw that day. But David had a huge secret
weapon that neither the people nor their opponents
or Goliath could see. David packed something might-
ier than a pistol. He possessed confidence in God.

So David killed the giant with just one stone because when he flung it with faith, God directed that
tiny rock to Goliath's forehead. David never would
have been able to do that with his own strength and
ability. But the shepherd boy's faith and confidence in
God filled him with something more: the promise of
God—the ability to win.

God wants to fill you with that same confidence.
All you have to do is choose faith in his power.

"But," you might say, "my giants are pretty big."
Maybe your debts are bigger than your year's paychecks, or maybe you don't even have paychecks right
now. Maybe your despair seems deeper than any hope
you've ever had. What then?

Do what David did when he faced Goliath. Do what another king did when a huge army started attacking him and his people.

When you don't know what to do, keep your eyes on the one who does.

Have you heard the story of Jehoshaphat?[9] Funny name, I know, but this guy was the king of Judah.

Jehoshaphat received bad news that a vast army was coming against him. Of course this caused alarm. But the first thing Jehoshaphat did was to seek the Lord. The king proclaimed a fast and began to ask God what in the world to do. He prayed, "God, we have no power to face this vast army that is attacking us. We don't know what to do, but our eyes are on you."

That's what unshakable confidence in God looks like. It looks like you fastening your gaze on God. It looks like you going to him in prayer. It looks like you taking heart that God will do what you can't—whatever that may be!

You know where this story is going. Jehoshaphat put his confidence in God, then God sent confusion into the enemy's camp. Those soldiers couldn't see straight. Their thinking was crazy, and they began to destroy one another instead of Jehoshaphat and his kingdom, which they'd come to seize.

Jehoshaphat didn't even have to fight the battle. God did it for him.

Persevere in Faith

The Bible says patient endurance is what you need. Right now, in the midst of adversity, is when you need to persevere.[10] Don't give up. Don't get discouraged. Right now you need to remain faithful, steadfast, and consistent.

You might want to insist, "I'm tired of waiting for things to change! I just want to give up!"

Okay. Insist. Say it. Get it out—each of us gets tired along life's way. We want to give up. We get ready to throw in the towel. God knows that. He can take it when you tell him these things. In fact he wants you to bring your discouragement to him and to give him your burdens.[11]

So tell him you want to give in—and then don't. Choose not to give up. Make the choice, even if you don't know how you're going to keep choosing. That is what faith is: you choose again and again and again without any guarantee or anything sure. Faith is not faith without blindly hoping, believing anyway, choosing to persevere when everything says to do otherwise.

"Be steadfast, unmovable, always abounding in the

work of the Lord," the Bible says.[12]

When I think of being unmovable I think of Stax, my friend Susan's English bulldog. Stax is a character who loves to ride on a skateboard, but his speedy antics stop when it comes to keeping an object in his mouth. That dog becomes a rock and a fighter. He won't budge and he won't give in. Every time he chomps on a toy, you might as well give up trying to pull it from him because he...

- **never wavers in stance.** He plants his back feet in a defense position and never moves them.
- **never lets go.** He uses the front part of his body to pull what he wants, then grips tight with his jaw and keeps on clamping.
- **sets his eyes on the object.** He is so focused that he's not affected by anything around him, not even a treat. (Susan says for Stax that's a miracle!)
- **remains unaffected by time.** He just keeps pulling until he gets the object of his desire.

When it comes to our faith, we need to have bulldog tenacity like Stax. We need to plant our feet in the Word of God, keep our eyes on the prize, never let go of the Word, and be patient as we wait on God's timing.

There is victory. For Stax, it is the toy or a treat. For us, the reward is so much more rich—our destiny.

Every promise takes persistence

Whenever I think about persistence, I think of Job in the Old Testament. Satan destroyed everything Job had, taking his family and trying to take his faith. But Job didn't give up; he didn't quit.[13] For one year, Satan continued to attack Job, taking his home and business, even his health.

Through trial after trial, Job remained steadfast.

All that persistence was followed by God's promise. God never left Job, and in the end he completely delivered Job from his trouble. In fact, God gave Job twice as much as he had before his troubles.

Twice as much. That's the kind of God we serve: the God who keeps a record of the wrongs and personal losses we have endured and gives us double for our trouble—double peace, double joy, double strength, double friends, double ideas. For Kevin and me, even double children—twins!

God richly rewarded Job, whom he loved, and whom the Bible tells of in this way: "You have heard of Job's perseverance and have seen what the Lord finally brought about…the Lord is full of compassion and is merciful."[14]

Persistent faith, persistent prayers, and persistent gratefulness prepare you for God's promises. The Bible says that it is through faith and patience that we inherit those promises.[15] And that is the next key in how to persist.

To receive the promise, practice patience

You have to wait patiently for God's timing, and in the waiting time God will do his work in your heart and life. He will develop you and mature you and enlarge you. He will never allow you to be tempted beyond what you are able to bear.[16]

Proverbs 19:11 says a man's wisdom gives him patience, and wisdom says: *I'm not going to get off course. I'm not going to grumble and complain. I'm going to keep my focus on God and the things of God.*

That is what Job did for most of that year of extreme suffering. Even when his friends told him to give up, to blame God or believe he was doing something wrong, Job chose to be patient. He chose to be wise. He knew that even when we can't feel God or see him at work or hear his voice, God is still with us. He is still watching. He is still directing our steps, when we choose to take each of those steps with a patient faith.[17]

That is the real race that the Bible talks about, the one you take with each patient step. The Bible says to run with perseverance the race that is marked out for you.[18] Don't quit—run and finish. No one else can do that for you. Only you can run your race. Only you can claim the prize, the promise God has planned with your name on it. And God is with you in the race. He stays *with* you and *in* you and *for* you. He has even hemmed you in, both behind you and before you.[19] He's got you covered.

To receive the promise, arise—and arise again

Sometimes perseverance is more a matter of endurance. I understand endurance. There were times when I wanted to give in to depression. I felt horrible. I couldn't see my way through. To persevere meant truly to endure. My mind and emotions wanted to give in to hopelessness. I had thoughts like: *My situation is hopeless. I cannot make it another day.*

I had to refuse to believe those thoughts and believe the truth: "I can make it! I have God's grace to make it!" I had to say those things a lot. I had to get up each depressing day and proclaim these promises to myself and to God, promises to persevere, to keep on…and in the process an interesting thing happened.

In time, the decision to arise again and again worked its wonders. My mornings began to come with hope, not despair, and beauty rather than the ashen gray of depression.

TO HELP YOU MORE

Eight Things God Promises

God loves you so much. He makes these eight promises for those who trust in him, and he even puts his Word on it. Take a look at these promises in the Bible:

1. **God is good and will bless you.** Psalm 34:8–9: "Oh, taste and see that the Lord is good; blessed is the man who trusts in him... there is no want to those who fear him."

2. **You are surrounded by mercy.** Psalm 32:10: "Many sorrows shall be to the wicked; but he who trusts in the Lord, mercy shall surround him."

3. **You will be fully redeemed.** Psalm 130:7: "Put your hope in the Lord, for with the Lord is unfailing love and with him is full redemption."

4. **God will give you the longings of your heart.** Psalm 37:4 (NLT): "Take delight in the Lord, and he will give you your heart's desires."

5. **You can be happy.** Proverbs 16:20: "He who

trusts in the Lord will be happy."

6. **You can delight in your life.** Psalm 36:7–8: "How precious is your lovingkindness, O God! Therefore the children of men put their trust under the shadow of your wings. They are abundantly satisfied with the fullness of your house, and you give them drink from the river of your pleasures."

7. **God will remove any shame from you.** Psalm 25:3: "No one who trusts in you will ever be disgraced."

8. **You will not be disappointed.** Isaiah 49:23: "Then you will know that I am the Lord; those who hope in me will not be disappointed."

God's love is everlasting and his rewards are rich. Who couldn't find joy in that?

God's ways always work. He tells us: "Arise [from the depression and prostration in which circumstances have kept you—rise to a new life]! Shine (be radiant with the glory of the Lord), for your light has come, and the glory of the Lord has risen upon you! Then you shall see and be radiant, and your heart shall thrill and tremble with joy [at the glorious deliverance] and be enlarged."[20]

Do your circumstances have you flat on the ground? Are you flat out, feeling exhausted, helpless, and completely overcome? That is the best place for you to say to God, "Help me." And it is the best place from which to rise. Everything will be more beautiful once you are up again, because the glory of the Lord will rise with you.

If you look up the word *glory* in the Hebrew language, it implies that his splendor, favor, and honor are heavy upon you. *Already upon you.*

When we are weak, God is strong in us. His grace will get us up and get us through.[21]

Do God's Will

Whatever you are dreaming of or praying about today, don't give up on those things. It's easy to fall into the trap of discouragement or hopelessness, but that's not God's will for you. Does that mean he will always answer your prayers and give you things in just the way you ask for them? No. But he has something great in mind for you. He has more in store for every day of life he's given you. In times of discouragement, remember these three truths:

God loves faithfulness so much that he'll get you to your breakthrough

What do you do when you feel like giving up, when you're weary from practicing patience and the challenges keep coming? Those are the times you simply obey. You choose to trust God. You don't give up on him even when you think he may have given up on you—because he hasn't. He won't. He will never forsake nor abandon you.[22]

The Bible reminds us what the will of God is: *Always be joyful. Keep on praying. No matter what happens, always be thankful, for this is God's will for you.*[23]

So when you don't know what to else to do, keep doing what you know to do from God's Word. You may not feel the effects in the midst of doing positive things, but keep doing them when it seems all the wrong things are happening to you. I remind myself often that the simple daily acts of faithful obedience make all the difference in the world. Things like:

- keeping a positive attitude of faith and expectancy.
- continuing to be grateful for what you do have.
- going to church where you can be encouraged weekly.
- surrounding yourself with godly friends.
- spending time with God every day.

- speaking faith-filled words over your life and destiny.
- holding your peace and knowing that God promises to fight your battles for you.
- being still and knowing that he is God.

Choose to press on, to keep doing what he wants you to do, and choose to believe his promise to you: *I hold victory in store for the upright. I am a shield to those whose walk is blameless, for I guard the course of the just and protect the way of my faithful ones.*[24]

God wants you to win so much that he sends heavenly help.

I love the story of Daniel in the Bible.[25] Daniel is beside himself. He needs help; his people need help. So he's doing the only things in his power at the moment. He's reading the Scriptures. He's praying to God for help. And do you know what happens as he prays?

The angel Gabriel appears. An angel. For real.

Gabriel, God's messenger, tells Daniel: "You who are highly esteemed, consider carefully the words I am about to speak to you, and stand up, for I have now been sent to you."

I don't know about you, but if an angel like Gabriel showed up right now and told me to stand up, I'd leap to attention like I leaped over that fence when that horse was chasing me!

That's exactly what Daniel did. The Bible tells us he stood up, trembling.

The angel was full of good news though. "Do not be afraid, Daniel," Gabriel said. "Since the first day that you set your mind to gain understanding and to humble yourself before your God, your words were heard, and I have come in response to them."[26]

There are four truths here for us today, and they all begin with how God sees the obedient heart:

1. **God highly esteems you.** This is the first thing Gabriel said to Daniel. That's how God sees you— highly esteemed. God loves you and watches over your life. He does not ignore nor neglect you.

2. **When you speak, God listens!** Gabriel said, "Your words were heard." Just because you don't get an immediate answer doesn't mean that God hasn't heard you. If you look deeper into the passage, Gabriel even explains to Daniel that he was detained for a while, but God was listening to Daniel all along and made sure help got to him.

3. **God dispatched the answer the first day that Daniel prayed.** When you pray in faith, God responds. The very day you pray, God dispatches the answer.

4. **We have backup!** Gabriel had been working be-

hind the scenes to get Daniel's answer to him. The Bible even tells us what Gabriel looked like: a man who was dressed in linen with a belt made of the finest gold and a body like chrysolite—arms and legs like burnished bronze and eyes like flaming torches, a voice like the sound of a multitude.[27] Wow. That's some pretty serious backup!

Again, note how there was a delay, and God let Daniel see that. See how God wants us to know what is happening in the unseen realm? Gabriel faced opposition in getting the answer to Daniel, but there were no worries because Gabriel got his cell phone out and called Michael, his fellow angel.

Mike, Gabe said, *I'm calling for backup! I need your help.*

And Michael came to his rescue.

Pretty amazing, isn't it? God's helping us with angels, whom he has helping one another…in order to help us. We are not alone! There are more powerful forces for us than against us.

What's so wonderful is Daniel got his answer because he didn't give up the first day or the first week or the second week or the third week of his trial. Daniel persevered until he got the answer. God is at work for each of us all the time—God loves his creation so.

What Daniel shows us is that we don't know what is happening behind the scenes. We do know that the day we pray, God begins to work on our behalf. What are you praying for today? A wayward, prodigal child? Better health? A job? To be free from an addiction? Don't quit until you get your answer—your answer is on the way.

God knows that sometimes faith is a fight

We are engaged in a battle and the enemy wants to steal your faith. He wants to steal your blessings and joy, your family and destiny—everything he can. But you have to fight the good fight of faith.

Paul compares the fight of faith to a race. He encourages us to fight the good fight, finish the race, keep the faith.[28]

> *God is at work for each of us all the time.*

When I speak to groups on this, I have a large banner that I place on the stage behind me that says FINISH LINE. I like people to have a visual picture of making it to the finish line.

Think about your race. Think about everything discouraging you right now, every heartbreak, loss, broken dream, unrealized hope. What is keeping you from keeping on, what is threatening to steal your joy, your faith today? How are you fighting it? Have you tried prayer? Are you reading God's Word? Are you still tempted to give in, to give up?

Now imagine that big finish line right in front of you.

Can you see your answer on the other side? Can you see your dream fulfilled? It's just ahead of you. This is not a time to give up. Maybe there are things going on behind you, or off to the side. Maybe you can't see because everything is just a little foggy when you're in a storm, or the wind is blowing too hard into your face. But can't you just feel how close you are to the finish line? What if, in obedience, in the fight for your life, you took one step? What if, not knowing anything of what God is up to around you or off to the sides or even ahead, you stepped out once more?

Faith Means You Don't Quit

More. That is what life with God is all about: more of life, more of him, more of the destiny he created for you.

Would you really quit when you may be just one step away from all that? How do you not know that the next step you take will be the one that gets you there?

God tells us: *Do not throw away your confidence! Don't shrink back! I will richly reward your faith! When you persevere—you will receive from me!*[29]

God wants you so much to chase him. He longs to give you, the apple of his eye, what he has promised. He tells us over and again in the Bible:

For I have loved you with an everlasting love.[30]

I have loved you.[31]

I love you.[32]

He doesn't want you to give up. He wants you to taste the sweetness of his promises—to bite, not into thin air, but into your destiny, to swallow it and live it, to feed off of him forever.

And all you have to do is take one step. And one more and then one more.

As God Makes You More

A Prayer for You

∽

Dear Heavenly Father,
I come to you just as I am and I know that you hear
me and accept me. I ask you to forgive me of all my
sins. I recognize that Jesus Christ, your Son, sacrificed
his life for me in order that I might have forgiveness,
eternal life, and abundant life on this earth. I accept
Jesus as my Lord and Savior. I desire to live for you
and fulfill the destiny that you have for me. I thank
you that I am your child and that you will direct my
steps into your perfect will.

I love you,

_____

*Name*_____

*Date*_____

Notes

Introduction

1. Song of Solomon 8:6 (New International Version).

1. Finding More When Things Explode

1. Proverbs 18:14.
2. John 10:29 (NIV).
3. Romans 8:28.
4. Psalm 121: 1–8, especially verses 3 and 4.
5. Psalm 121; Isaiah 41:10.
6. Psalm 139:7–12.

2. Finding More When You Feel Flawed

1. Psalm 103:3.

2. Psalm 139.
3. Ephesians 1:11 (NIV); Ephesians 2:10 (New Living Translation).
4. Genesis 1.
5. Ephesians 2:10 (NLT).
6. 1 Corinthians 10:13.
7. Psalm 37:23–24 (NIV).
8. Psalm 90:12 (New King James Version).
9. Ephesians 1:17–19 (*The Message*).
10. James 1:5.
11. Exodus 6:10–13.
12. Proverbs 19:21.
13. Galatians 5:7 (*The Message*).
14. Psalm 25:12.
15. Philippians 3:3.
16. Ephesians 1:11.
17. Ephesians 2:10.
18. 2 Kings 6–7.
19. Proverbs 3:5–6 (NLT).
20. Revelation 19:14 (NLT).

3. Finding More When People Fail You

1. Genesis 37–47.
2. Proverbs 27:6; Psalm 141:5; Ephesians 4:15.
3. 1 Corinthians 2:9 (NLT).
4. Acts 7:9–10.

5. Philippians 4:13.
6. 2 Corinthians 12:9.
7. Jeremiah 29:11.
8. Psalm 25:3.

4. Finding More When You're Distracted

1. Psalm 37:4; Psalm 20:4.
2. Proverbs 29:18.
3. 2 Timothy 1:6.
4. Romans 8:28.
5. Jeremiah 29:11–14.
6. Habakkuk 2:2–3 (NKJV).
7. Ibid.
8. Luke 4:17–19.
9. Ibid.
10. Habakkuk 2:2.
11. James 1:6–7.
12. Psalm 78:19.
13. Romans 10:17.
14. Mark 11:24; Matthew 12:37.
15. Proverbs 13:3.
16. Philippians 4:19.
17. Judges 14:6.
18. Isaiah 55:8.
19. John 14:23 (Amplified Bible).
20. John 2:5 (NKJV).

21. Psalm 32:8 (NLT).
22. Genesis 4:1–16.
23. 1 Samuel 18–31.
24. James 3:16.
25. Hebrews 6:12.
26. Galatians 6:9.
27. 2 Corinthians 1:4.

5. Finding More When You're Heartbroken

1. Philippians 1:6; Psalm 138:8.
2. Philippians 1:6 (The Message).
3. Genesis 37.
4. Genesis 39.
5. Genesis 39:19–41:49.
6. Genesis 41.
7. Hebrew 13:5–6; Romans 8:31–39; 2 Corinthians 4:7–11.
8. Psalm 103:4.
9. Galatians 6:9.
10. Pastor Tommy Barnett of Phoenix First Assembly of God.
11. Ibid.
12. Ibid.
13. Isaiah 55:9.
14. Jeremiah 29:11.

15. Psalm 37:23.
16. Proverbs 3:5–6 (*The Message*).

6. Finding More When You're Afraid

1. Isaiah 41:10 (NIV).
2. Proverbs 23:7 (NKJV).
3. Robert Yehling, "Mind of the Body," *Science of Mind* (December 2004). Found online at http://www.drgmrandall.com/Mind%20of %20the%20Body.pdf.
4. Romans 12:2 (NLT).
5. 1 John 4:18.
6. Joshua 1:9.
7. Proverbs 15:15 (Amplified Bible).
8. Psalm 34:8.
9. Psalm 23:6.
10. Psalm 91:9–12.
11. Isaiah 41:13.
12. Hebrews 13:20.
13. John 14:16.
14. Isaiah 43:5.
15. Psalm 34:4 (NLT).
16. Ephesians 5:15–16.
17. Philippians 4:13 (NASV).
18. John 14:1 (Amplified Bible).
19. Matthew 28:20; Hebrews 13:5–6.

20. Matthew 6:25–34.
21. Psalm 46:10.
22. Proverbs 3:5.
23. Isaiah 43:1–3; Jeremiah 29:11–13.
24. Philippians 4:6-7.
25. Joshua 1:9 (NIV).
26. Ibid.
27. 2 Timothy 1:7.
28. Isaiah 43:2.
29. Psalm 56:11.
30. Luke 21:26.
31. Mark 5:21–42.

7. Finding More When You're Disappointed

1. John 16:33 (Amplified Bible).
2. Ibid.
3. John 10:10.
4. Hebrews 6:19.
5. Psalm 33:18.
6. 1 Thessalonians 5:23.
7. Colossians 1:9.
8. 1 Corinthians 10:13.
9. Psalm 121:1–2.
10. Jeremiah 29:11.
11. James 4:8.

12. Deuteronomy 29:29.

13. 2 Corinthians 1:4 (NIV).

14. Psalm 73:16.

15. Isaiah 26:3.

16. Mark 10:27.

17. Psalm 127:3.

18. I highly recommend the books, practical advice, and spiritual counsel of Dr. Reginald Cherry for going through the emotional issues I experienced. You can learn more about him and his work at his Pathway to Healing website: www.thepathwaytohealing.com.

19. Psalm 40:2; Isaiah 61:3.

20. 2 Corinthians 4:17–18 (Amplified Bible).

21. Psalm 18:30.

22. Psalm 25:3.

8. Finding More When You Can't Let Go

1. Isaiah 43:18–19.

2. Philippians 3:13–15.

3. Romans 8:35–37.

4. Isaiah 43:25 (NIV Study Bible).

5. From the gift booklet *I Am Woman, I Am Invincible, I Am Tired…* by Born to Shop © 2006, Peter Pauper Press. Found online at http://www.peterpauper.com/advanced_search_result.php

?keywords=born+to+shop&search_in
_description=1 and onamazon.com at http
://www.amazon.com/Woman-Invincible
-Tired-Keepsake-Humor/dp/1593599331
/ref=sr_1_1?ie=UTF8&s= book&qid
=1301517238&sr=8-1.

6. Genesis 4:1–16.
7. Genesis 27:1–17.
8. Numbers 12:1.
9. 2 Samuel 13:1–22.
10. 1 Corinthians 13:7 (Amplified Bible).
11. Proverbs 11:17.
12. Guideposts ©1972 Carmel, NY 10512
   (www.guideposts.com).
13. Ibid.
14. Matthew 10:8 and Matthew 5:7.
15. Psalm 147:3
16. Isaiah 61:1–3.

9. Finding More When You've Been Labeled

1. Mark 10:46–52.
2. Jeremiah 1:5.
3. Jeremiah 1:7.
4. 1 Chronicles 4:9–10.
5. Ibid.

6. Ibid.
7. James 4:3 and John 5:14.
8. 1 Chronicles 4:9–10.
9. Isaiah 41:10; Romans 8:38–39.
10. Romans 12:1 (NIV).
11. Joel 3:10.
12. John 1:12; Romans 8:17; Ephesians 1:3.
13. Ephesians 2:10; Colossians 2:10.
14. 1 Samuel 16:7.
15. Ephesians 1:3–4; 1 Thessalonians 1:4.
16. Romans 12:6; 1 Peter 4:10; 1 Timothy 4:12–13.
17. 1 Timothy 4:14
18. Ephesians 1:3–8.
19. Isaiah 43:4.
20. Psalm 139:14.
21. Psalm 17:8.
22. Psalm 5:12.
23. Deuteronomy 28:1–14.
24. Psalm 1:3.
25. Acts 17:26–27.

10. Finding More When You Fail

1. Hebrews 4:15.
2. Hebrews 4:16 (*The Message*).
3. Paul J. Meyer, *Unlocking Your Legacy: 25 Keys for Success* (Chicago: Moody Publishers, 2003).

4. Luke 22:31.
5. Hebrews 7:25.
6. Psalm 103:8.
7. Genesis 3.
8. Matthew 7:20.
9. James 2:13; 1 Corinthians 13:8; 1 Peter 4:8.
10. John 8:3–11.
11. Matthew 7:12.
12. Bishop Dale Bronner of Word of Faith Family Worship Cathedral in Austell, Georgia.
13. Proverbs 24:16.
14. Ephesians 2:10.

11. Finding More When You Feel Unable

1. Hebrews 12:1, 13:20–21.
2. Romans 8:28 (Amplified Bible).
3. Exodus 4:10.
4. Luke 19:1–4.
5. Ephesians 2:1–7.
6. John 14:16–18 (Amplified Bible).
7. John 14:16, 14:26, 16:7.
8. 1 Corinthians 2:9–16; 1 John 2:27.
9. John 7:37–39; 1 John 2:1.
10. John 14:16–18; 1 Corinthians 2:1–5.
11. Romans 8:26.
12. John 14:26, 16:7–8; 1 John 2:1.

13. John 14:16 (Amplified Bible).
14. John 15:16 (NIV).
15. 2 Corinthians 5:20 (NIV).
16. Colossians 3:17.
17. Psalm 139:13–16; Romans 12:4–6; Ephesians 1:3.
18. 1 Corinthians 6:19.
19. 1 John 2:27.
20. Ephesians 6:10–20.
21. Luke 4:1–3.
22. Luke 4:17–19.
23. 2 Corinthians 1:21–22 (NIV).
24. 1 Thessalonians 2:4.
25. 2 Corinthians 12:10.
26. 1 Corinthians 3:1–5 (Amplified Bible).
27. 2 Corinthians 10:12.

12. Finding More When You're Ready to Give Up

1. Psalm 3:5.
2. 1 Corinthians 10:13.
3. Hebrews 12:1–2.
4. Hebrews 10:35–37.
5. 1 Corinthians 1:9; Malachai 3:6.
6. Acts 2:25–28 (*The Message*).
7. 1 John 5:14.

8. 1 Samuel 17:20–54.
9. 2 Chronicles 20.
10. Hebrews 10:35–37.
11. Matthew 11:28–30.
12. 1 Corinthians 15:58 (NIV).
13. Job 1–2.
14. James 5:11.
15. Hebrews 6:11–14.
16. 1 Corinthians 10:13 (NIV).
17. Proverbs 3:5–6 and 2 Corinthians 5:7.
18. Hebrews 12:1.
19. Psalm 139:5.
20. Isaiah 60:1, 5 (Amplified Bible); Deuteronomy 31:6; Hebrews 13:5 (NIV).
21. 2 Corinthians 12:9.
22. Hebrews 13:5–6.
23. 1 Thessalonians 5:16–18.
24. Proverbs 2:7–21.
25. Daniel 9:1–3.
26. Ibid.
27. Daniel 10:5–6.
28. 2 Timothy 4:7.
29. Hebrews 10:35–39.
30. Jeremiah 31:3.
31. John 14:21; John 15:9–10.
32. John 3:16.

Acknowledgments

Writing this book has been a journey taken with the help of many friends, loved ones, and family members. I am eternally grateful for the wonderful people instrumental in making this project enjoyable and memorable.

Many thanks to Rolf Zettersten and Jana Burson, our friends at FaithWords for helping make my dream come true.

I am grateful for our friends, Jan Miller and Shannon Marven at Dupree/Miller, for believing in this project, and me, and for their hard work in making it possible

I am blessed to have worked with Jeanette Thomason, who is incredibly gifted and who helped make this book what it is.

I am immensely grateful for my husband, Kevin, and our three children, Catherine, Caroline, and

Christopher, for unending support. I couldn't have made it without your love, encouragement, and patience. I love and treasure each of you with all my heart.

Thank you to my Daddy, who always saw the best in me and inspired me to live with courage and boldness. Thank you to my mother, Dodie Osteen, for your example as a wife, mother, and grandmother. You are a remarkable lady.

A heartfelt thanks to my brother, Joel Osteen, for giving me wisdom and direction in writing this book. You continue to inspire, teach, and encourage me, and I greatly admire and respect you. I am so proud of you and Victoria.

Thank you to my siblings: Dr. Paul Osteen, Tamara Graff, and April Simons and your families. You are each amazing and incredibly gifted. I am honored to be your sister.

Special thanks to my "A Team": Emily Davila, Irene Franco, Elizabeth Ortega, Gabriela Ferrel, Conchi Revelo, and Ana Diaz for your encouragement, prayer support, and labors of love. I know you always have my back.

Thank you, Bebe Hackney, for always being there for me over the last thirty years. I treasure your friendship.

I am grateful for friends and mentors who have influenced my life in an enormous way. Thank you,

Billy and Marilyn Morrison, for your leadership, friendship, and fellowship as a teenager. Thank you, Kathleen Taylor, for being a friend, encourager, and prayer partner when I was devastated by divorce. Thank you, Phyllis Sitton, Lois Godwin, and Renee Branson for being there for me during the mail bomb explosion, and for your love and example throughout my life.

A special thank you to Debra George for wisdom, love, prayer, and friendship over the last twenty-five years. I am thankful for your support and help in editing this book.

Thank you to our Lakewood staff and family for loyalty to the Lord and to our family. This is an amazing gift that has carried me, and your fellowship, in turn, carries others. May we continue to be about the Lord's work together.

Finding Yourself in This Book

God Is Making Me More

This section is designed to help you find, chapter by chapter, what more God has in mind for you. Use it to make notes, confide longings and hopes and fears, or log prayers about what God is saying specifically to you as you read. Spend time talking or journaling to God about what you learn, or discuss these things with a confidential friend. As God works in your life to lead you toward your purpose for him, look back on these notes and see how he's been using every event and circumstance to make you more today than you were yesterday—and how he's leading you into your destiny.

1. Finding More When Things Explode

Explosive events in my life:

_____

_____

What more I need or want in these situations:

_____

Things God is doing today to pick up the pieces:

_____

_____

Where I need you, God, to help me reach my destiny:

_____

_____

My hopes are...

_____

_____

2. Finding More When You Feel Flawed

I see my flaws as:

_____

_____

I'm getting stuck in this way by this flaw:

_____

_____

How I think God sees me, what he loves about me:

_____

_____

Where I need you, God, to remind me of what you created in me, with me, for me:

_____

_____

I would describe the masterpiece I want to be as looking and acting like and being…

_____

_____

3. Finding More When People Fail You

I've been hurt most by this person, and I feel they failed me in this way:

_____

_____

This relationship changed me in these ways (from what, to what):

_____

In this relationship, I learned:

_____

Where I need you, God, to heal me from the hurts of this relationship:

_____

_____

My desires in relationships are…

_____

_____

4. Finding More When You're Distracted

These events paralyzed me emotionally and left me
in limbo land once (and when that was):

_____

_____

If certain things hadn't happened to me, I wish I
could:

_____

_____

I could still move toward my heart's desire if God
were to (do, say, show):

_____

_____

I need you, God, to focus my heart and energy on
these things:

_____

_____

My sense of what you, God, are calling me to do and
be is…

_____

I can do these things today, this week, this month, to
move me toward your purpose for me:

_____

_____

5. Finding More When You're Heartbroken

My dream has been:

_____

_____

I've held on to (or let go of) this dream because:

_____

_____

I can take these steps to move closer to my dream:

_____

_____

Where I need you, God, to help me grasp my dream:

_____

_____

My palace (place of my heart's desire) looks like...

_____

_____

6. Finding More When You're Afraid

Fears and worries I'm wrestling with right now include:

_____

_____

Why I'm afraid, anxious, or worried:

_____

_____

What would happen if I pushed through my fear and each time I felt anxious chose to give that to God and plunge forward:

_____

_____

Where I need you, God, to help me hand my fears to you:

_____

_____

My fearless life would look like this:

_____

_____

7. Finding More When You're Disappointed

Disappointments I'm dealing with now are…

_____

My expectations were:

_____

I long to do or be or have this, God, because:

_____

Where I need you, God, to help me see your purpose in this:

_____

_____

My disappointment can help me (appoints me) to help others in this way...

_____

Thank you, God, for giving me this appointment because...

_____

_____

8. Finding More When You Can't Let Go

I've been hanging onto these things:

_____

The thing(s) I'm hanging onto are affecting me in at least these three ways:

_____

If I were to let go of these things, this might happen:

_____

God, I need you to help me let go of these things:

Replace the things I've held onto, God, with:

_____

_____

9. Finding More When You've Been Labeled

I've been labeled this way before:

_____

_____

This label troubles me most because:

_____

How I think God would label me today:

_____

_____

How I want him to label me when I get to where he wants me to be:

_____

_____

Where I need you, God, to help me see where you're taking me, how you want to label me:

_____

_____

When I receive a new name as God has promised (Revelation 2:12), I would like it to be (and because)…

_____

_____

10. Finding More When You Fail

I've failed in this area:

_____

I see my other failures as…

_____

_____

What distresses me most about my failures:

_____

Where I need you, God, to release me from my failures is…

_____

Today I can be an overcomer and not overcome in these ways (list three steps you can take):

_____

11. Finding More When You Feel Unable

I've been made to feel unable in this area:

_____

_____

I wish, God, I were better equipped to...

_____

_____

I'm getting stuck in this way by my thinking on what I am equipped with or not:

_____

_____

Where I need you, God, to show me my assignment in life is:

_____

_____

I know I am approved by you, God, because...

_____

_____

I wish to sense you choosing me, God, in this area:

_____

_____

As your chosen one I would like to do this more than anything:

_____

_____

12. Finding More When You're Ready to Give Up

I've wanted to give up or quit in this area because:

_____

_____

This might happen if I gave up:

_____

I can do this today to increase my faith, knowing you have the perfect timing in mind for me:

_____

_____

Where I need you, God, to help me stay strong and keep on is…

_____

_____

The race I'm running looks like this:

_____

_____

What I want to hear you say and how I imagine you at my finish line is…

_____

_____

Readers' Group Discussion Guide

1. In chaos, who and what do you tend to focus upon first? How do you sense God is near (or not)? What draws you to him when things implode in your life?
2. People talk about the *Mona Lisa*'s mysterious smile. How would you like to appear in God's masterpiece painting of you? What do you wish others saw about you that you know God loves?
3. What things have helped you most in working through the pain of someone failing you? What pains you most when you fail someone?
4. How has (or can) a heartache in your life prepare you to serve others? What makes a wounded healer more effective (or not)?
5. What have you done with a broken or lingering dream? How do you tend it? What can you do today to nurture that dream and reach it—how do you stir it?

6. Lisa points out how aggressively fear can take hold of you. In what aggressive ways can you fight your particular fears? What would refusing to fear mean in your most anxious areas? Describe three situations and what actions you could take to refuse fear.

7. In your own disappointments how do you run to God (and not from him)? What does this look like in your life? What do you do? How does it affect you?

8. What are you struggling to let go of these days— a relationship, a job situation, an emotional issue? What might you be able to grab hold of by letting go of past hurts, disappointments, frustrations? What's stopping you from letting go? What would help you?

9. What label do you most wish to wear and why? How can you put on that label today—what would you need to do or become?

10. How do you react to someone else's failure? How do you wish others would react to your failure? What good can come out of an area where you've failed? Or where someone else has failed? Think about three things God can do to redeem the situation(s) or person(s).

11. When have you been surprised that you were made of more than you thought—that you were able to do something you didn't previously think

possible? How did that change you? When have you experienced a moment of sensing you were specifically chosen to carry on a particular mission?

12. What makes you want to give up? What makes you want to keep on? How can you summon those things that keep you persevering the next time you feel like quitting something?

About Lisa Osteen Comes

Lisa Osteen Comes is associate pastor at Lakewood Church in Houston, Texas, the largest church in the United States.

Well known for her practical, easy-to-understand messages, she is no stranger to the extraordinary. She's survived both a birth defect and a mail bomb explosion that made headlines around the world, and she has overcome many other challenges with hope and optimism. She speaks to Lakewood and thousands viewing its services via broadcasts around the world.

She and her husband, Kevin, live in Houston with their three children, Catherine, Caroline, and Christopher.

For more about Lisa's latest activities, to read her blog, and to sign up to receive her free, weekly Inbox Inspiration e-mails, visit her website: www.lisacomes.com. You can also find her on Facebook and Twitter as Lisa Osteen Comes.